THE BEST
W**I**NES
IN THE
S**U**PER
MARKETS
2011

THE BEST
W🍷NES
IN THE
S🍷PER
MARKE🍷S
2011

NED HALLEY

foulsham
LONDON • NEW YORK • TORONTO • SYDNEY

foulsham

The Oriel, Thames Valley Court, 183-187 Bath Road, Slough, Berkshire, SL1 4AA, England

Foulsham books can be found in all good bookshops and direct from **www.foulsham.com**

ISBN: 978-0-572-03599-0

Printed and bound in Great Britain by Martins the Printers

Contents

Relative values

I must start this new edition with an explanation of my scoring system. All the wines described are rated on a scale of 0 to 10. I write these numbers down alongside my notes when tasting, and most of the wines scoring 8 or more are included in this book. But these marks are principally an indicator of relative value. I'm not trying to suggest that Sainsbury's non-vintage House Côtes du Rhône at £3.69, which I have given 10 because I think it's unbeatable of its kind at the price, would be preferable to Marks & Spencer's St Aubin 1er Cru Les Charmois 2006 at £17.99, which scores 9. What I'm saying is that if all I had to spend was £3.69 I would not hesitate to spend it on the Sainsbury's bargain, while I would be slightly more equivocal (only very slightly, mind you) about blowing my last £17.99 on the M&S burgundy.

Am I making sense? The point about The Best Wines in the Supermarkets is that it is a guide to what is actually there, on the shelf. I'm working on the principle that most customers are shopping on a budget. What's the best value for the money you have? That's why the listings are arranged in ascending price order. You use this book by looking up the supermarket of your choice, and under that heading check out the wine offering, which is arranged by colour, then nation by nation. Each wine is described as well as marked, so you know not just how much I liked it, but why.

All the wines mentioned are recommended. If they score 6 or 7, as a small number do, it means I have liked the wine but have doubts about the price, or believe that while the wine is not entirely to my own taste, I can see it might appeal to others. A score of 8 signifies a very good wine at a fair price and a score of 9 indicates special quality and value. Those that earn 10 out of 10 are, obviously enough, the wines I don't think can be bettered for the money.

The choice of wines at every price level in most supermarkets is overwhelming. Although the business is dominated by global brands – the likes of Arniston Bay, Echo Falls, Gallo and Hardys – the retail giants nevertheless continue to offer great numbers of alternative wines, even though they sell in small quantities by comparison. And they persist, too, with 'premium' wines, as bottles costing upwards of £7 are known in the trade, even though sales of these account for less than five per cent of the total retail market.

For those of us who enjoy the diversity of wine, it's a great mercy. The supermarkets are blamed, quite rightly, for the demise of the high-street merchants who used to offer the best ranges, so the least they can do is compensate us for this loss by offering decent selections of their own.

At this, some of the chains are doing very well indeed. In 2010, I have been mightily taken with the growing variety of 'own brand' wines that are exclusive to the retailer in question. Marks & Spencer leads the way here, because its entire range is sold under its own labels. Many of the wines are made by or under the supervision of M&S experts, and no other chain comes close in this respect.

Own-label ranges elsewhere are nevertheless impressive. This year Tesco celebrates ten years of its 'Finest' range, now extending to 100 different wines, and at the celebration tasting held in July, I could only wonder at the width of the diversity and the depth of quality. Asda, meanwhile, is being much garlanded in the annual awards schemes for its 'Extra Special' wines, which have introduced a distinctive new level of interest into an own-label range formerly renowned more for utilitarian value than anything else.

It is Sainsbury's, oddly enough, that has been the most creative at the value end of the market this year. Its brand new 'House' range, launched in the stores in June 2010, comprises about 20 different reds, whites and rosés, all non-vintage and starting at the unbelievably low price, for the Soave, of £3.29. Most are under £4 and the quality is consistently high across the range – and in some cases exceptional. It is, I suppose, a reflection of the hard times faced by wine producers – demand for cheaper wine has slumped during this long recession – in dealing with ruthless UK supermarkets, but from the similarly hard-pressed consumer's point of view it is surely very welcome indeed.

Bargain wines are being squeezed. With the present punitive excise duty on still wine of £1.61 per 75cl plus the VAT at 17.5% (rising to 20% in January 2011), just on the duty, the bottle price now starts at £1.89 before you get anything at all. Trade estimates put the minimum packaging and transport costs per bottle at 62p, and the typical retail margin at 25 per cent, which puts the value of the wine in a £3.99 bottle at 48p, a £4.99 bottle at 90p, a £5.99 bottle at £1.61, and a £6.99 bottle at £2.32.

Bearing in mind that wines costing under £7 account for just over 95 per cent of total retail sales, it's a wonder that the business is as important to supermarkets as it clearly is. And in spite of everything, the trade is growing. We continue to spend more on wine year by year, in spite of continuing economic gloom. True, most of the increased spend goes to the Treasury in tax revenues, and the rise in wine consumption coincides with a dramatic fall in beer sales, but it does look as if wine is here to stay, whatever the taxman, the health lobby and the Association of Chief Police Officers might say or do to eliminate it.

Which leads me to the curious question of the minimum pricing of alcoholic beverages. It's a policy idea credited to the Scottish Parliament, which so far has been unable to raise a majority of members' votes in favour, in spite of its averred purpose of pricing liquor beyond the reach of Scotland's legion problem drinkers. It is still, however, a live issue for the

Westminster government, whose former Chief Medical Officer Sir Liam Donaldson has espoused the cause. Sir Liam, who took up his very substantial NHS pension entitlement in the summer of 2010, has vowed to continue in his retirement to campaign for minimum pricing until the measure becomes law.

Wine lovers should perhaps contemplate the potential consequences of the policy Sir Liam so avidly supports. The principle of minimum pricing – let's call it MP for short – is this: all alcoholic drinks are rated in 'units', each of 1 centilitre of ethanol, or pure alcohol. Licensed retailers will be told they cannot sell any alcoholic drink at a price below X per unit. The figure mooted is 50p.

Sir Liam has pointed out that some alcoholic beverages currently retail for as little as 11p per unit. White cider, super-strength lagers, tonic wines and the like could thereby be hiked in price by a factor of up to five. Maybe problem drinkers would still try to find the money, but the bottom would soon fall out of the market. The offending products would no longer be viable.

How would this policy affect the price of wine? You might be surprised. A standard 75cl bottle at 12.5 per cent alcohol by volume (abv), typical for European wines, contains 9.375 units. To conform to MP it would therefore have to cost at least £4.69. A bottle at 14 per cent abv, common among New World wines, has 10.5 units, taking the MP up to £5.25.

There will, obviously, be no impact on wines already priced above these levels. But for wine lovers on more modest budgets – and that's most of us – it's a chilly prospect. The average price paid for a bottle of wine for drinking at home in Britain is currently about £4.30. In supermarkets, where we buy seven out of every ten bottles, it's nearer £4.10.

Under MP, such prices will be history. But look on the bright side. Dismal wines currently sold at a standard price below £4 will disappear. When you're paying at least £4.69, you'll expect something decent. Perhaps we can look forward to an era when the cheapest wines are not just MP, but also

MQ – minimum quality. With guaranteed minimum price levels (assuming the Government doesn't take all the uplift in tax, which it might), producers would be well-placed to lift standards in their vineyards and wineries.

There would also be an incentive for producers to examine the alcohol levels in their wines. Australian wines are very often even higher than 14 per cent, which is natural enough when working with super-ripe grapes. But viticultural technology could undoubtedly cope with reducing those levels. And European winemakers will surely welcome the prospect of some sort of advantage over the hot-climate competition, which bodes well for wine diversity.

These are not, I suppose, consequences that will have occurred to Sir Liam Donaldson, but in view of his ambitions for the years ahead, I guess wine lovers everywhere might like to wish him a long and happy retirement.

As always in introducing a new edition, I must apologise in advance for any price changes to wines made between going to press and publication. In view of the frequent increases in taxation of the last year or so and perpetual currency fluctuations, I can only hope that the long-term trend in this respect of supermarkets mysteriously maintaining as many prices as they do will continue for the foreseeable future. But don't hold your breath.

And finally, let me add that everything I say in this book about the wines and about the retailers is based on nothing more than my own knowledge and understanding. Taste in all things is personal, and more so in wine than in other respects. Here's to wine!

Following the announcement in the emergency budget of June 2010, VAT rises from 17.5 to 20 per cent in January 2011. The notional shelf price of a wine at £5 net of VAT consequently increases from £5.88 to £6.00.

Does it matter where it comes from?

This book categorises the wines by nation of origin. This is largely to follow the manner in which retailers arrange their wines, but also because it is the country or region of origin that still most distinguishes one style of wine from another. True, wines are now commonly labelled most prominently with their constituent grape variety, but to classify all the world's wines into the small number of principal grape varieties would make for categories of an unwieldy size.

Chardonnay, Sauvignon Blanc and Pinot Grigio are overwhelmingly dominant among whites, and four grapes – Cabernet Sauvignon, Grenache, Merlot and Syrah (also called Shiraz) – account for a high proportion of red wines made worldwide.

But each area of production still – in spite of creeping globalisation – puts its own mark on its wines. Chardonnays from France remain (for the moment at least) quite distinct from those of Australia. Cabernet Sauvignon grown in a cool climate such as that of Bordeaux is a very different wine from Cabernet cultivated in the cauldron of the Barossa.

Of course there are 'styles' that winemakers worldwide seek to follow. Yellow, oaky Chardonnays of the type pioneered in South Australia are now made in South Africa, too – and in new, high-tech wineries in New Zealand and Chile, Spain and Italy. But the variety is still wide. Even though the 'upfront' high-alcohol wines of the New World have grabbed so much of the market, France continues to make the elegant wines it has always made in its classic regions. Germany still produces racy, delicate Rieslings, and the distinctive zones of Italy, Portugal and Spain make ever more characterful wines from indigenous grapes, as opposed to imported global varieties.

Among less expensive wines, the theme is, admittedly, very much a varietal one. The main selling point for most 'everyday' wines is the grape of origin rather than the country of origin. It makes sense, because the characteristics of various grape varieties do a great deal to identify taste. A bottle of white wine labelled 'Chardonnay' can reasonably be counted on to deliver that distinctive peachy or pineappley smell and soft, unctuous apple flavours. A Sauvignon Blanc should evoke gooseberries, green fruit and grassy freshness. And so on.

For all the domination of Chardonnay and Cabernet, there are plenty of other grape varieties making their presence felt. Argentina, for example, has revived the fortunes of several French and Italian varieties that had become near-extinct at home. And the grape that (in my view) can make the most exciting of white wines, the Riesling, is now doing great things in the southern hemisphere as well as at home in Germany.

Among the current market trends, the rise of rosé continues apace. Now accounting for one out of every eight bottles of still wine sold, the choice of pink brands has simply exploded. I have certainly found a greater number of interesting pinks than might have been imagined a few years ago, but there are still plenty of dull ones with suspiciously high levels of residual sugar, so choose carefully.

Rosé wines are supposed to be made from black-skinned grapes. After the crush, the skins are left in contact with the juice for long enough to impart a pleasing colour, and maybe some flavour with it, and the liquids and solids are then separated before the winemaking process continues as it would for white wine.

Some rosés are made merely by blending red and white wines together. Oddly enough, this is how all (bar one or two) pink champagnes are made, as permitted under the local appellation rules. But under prevailing regulations in Europe, the practice is otherwise forbidden. Elsewhere in the world, where winemaking is very much less strictly standardised, blending is no doubt common enough.

It is, I know, a perpetual source of anguish to winemakers in tightly regulated European nations that they have to compete in important markets like Britain with producers in Australia, the Americas and South Africa who can make and label their wines just as they please. Vineyard irrigation, the use of oak chips, and the blending in of wines from other continents are all permitted in the New World and eschewed in the Old.

But would we have it any other way? No winemaker I have met in Bordeaux or Barolo, Bernkastel or Rias Baixas seriously wants to abandon the methods and conventions that make their products unique – even with an eye on creating a global brand. And in this present difficult economic climate for wine drinkers (and winemakers) worldwide, this assurance of enduring diversity is a comfort indeed.

Spot the grape

The character of most wines is defined largely by the grape variety, and it is a source of innocent pleasure to be able to identify which variety it is without peeking at the label. Here are some of the characteristics to look for in wines from the most widely planted varieties.

White

Chardonnay: Colour from pale to straw gold. Aroma can evoke peach, pineapple, sweet apple. Flavours of sweet apple, with creaminess or toffee from oak contact.

Fiano: Italian variety said to have been cultivated from ancient Roman times in the Campania region of southern Italy. Now widely planted on the mainland and in Sicily, it makes dry but soft wines of colours ranging from pale to pure gold with aromas of honey, orchard fruit, almonds and candied apricot. Well-made examples have beautifully balanced nutty-fresh flavours. Fiano is becoming fashionable.

Pinot Grigio: In its home territory of northeast Italy, it makes wines of pale colour, and pale flavour too. What makes the wine so popular might well be its natural low acidity. Better wines are more aromatic, even smoky, and pleasingly weighty in the manner of the Pinot Gris made in Alsace – now being convincingly imitated in both Argentina and New Zealand.

Riesling: In German wines, pale colour, sharp-apple aroma, racy fruit whether dry or sweet. Faint spritz common in young wines. Petrolly hint in older wines. Australian and New Zealand Rieslings have more colour and weight, and often a minerally, limey twang.

Sauvignon Blanc: In the dry wines, pale colour with suggestions of green. Aromas of asparagus, gooseberries, nettles, seagrass. Green, grassy fruit.

Semillon: Colour can be rich yellow. Aromas of tropical fruit including pineapple and banana. Even in dry wines, hints of honey amid fresh, fruit-salad flavours.

Viognier: Intense pale-gold colour. Aroma evokes apricots, blanched almonds and fruit blossom. Flavours include candied fruits. Finish often low in acidity.

Red

Cabernet Sauvignon: Dense colour, purple in youth. Strong aroma of blackcurrants and cedar wood ('cigar box'). Flavour concentrated, often edged with tannin so it grips the mouth.

Grenache: Best known in the Côtes du Rhône, it tends to make red wines pale in colour but forceful in flavour with a wild, hedgerow-fruit style and hints of pepper.

Merlot: Dark, rich colour. Aroma of sweet black cherry. Plummy, rich, mellow fruit can be akin to Cabernet but with less tannin. May be hints of bitter chocolate.

Pinot Noir: Colour distinctly pale, browning with age. Aromas of strawberry and raspberry. Light-bodied wine with soft-fruit flavours but dry, clean finish.

Sangiovese: The grape of Chianti and now of several other Italian regions, too. Colour is fine ruby, and may be relatively light; a plummy or even pruny smell is typical, and flavours can evoke blackcurrant, raspberry and nectarine. Tannin lingers, so the wine will have a dry, nutskin-like finish.

Shiraz or **Syrah:** Intense, near-black colour. Aroma of ripe fruit, sometimes spicy. Robust, rich flavours, commonly with high alcohol, but with soft tannins. The Shiraz of Australia is typically much more substantial than the Syrah of the south of France.

Tempranillo: Colour can be pale, as in Rioja. Blackcurrant aroma, often accompanied by vanilla from oak ageing. Tobacco, even leather, evoked in flavours.

There is more about all these varieties, and many others, in 'What Wine Words Mean' starting on page 121.

Looking for a
—— *favourite wine?* ——

If you have a favourite supermarket wine and hope to find it in this book, check the index starting on page 171.

The index is the most sensible place to start, because many of the wines I have tasted from any given supermarket, and thus entered under that chain's heading, will also be available from one or more of its rivals. I know, for example, that the very likeable Chilean red Errazuriz Merlot 2009 is sold by Asda at £7.98, but can also be found on the shelves of other retailers. I have listed it under Asda because that's where I tasted it, and to replicate this entry along with many others that are widely stocked, under all the relevant retailers, would crowd the pages with repetitions.

So, if you're interested in a branded wine you remember seeing in, say, Morrisons, don't look only in the very brief entry for that company. Check the index for the wine, and it might just be listed under another retailer's section.

Pick of the year

Out of the countless wines I have tasted over the year, 36 have scored the maximum 10 out of 10. Listed overleaf, the still wines range in price from a bit under £4 to a handful over £12, but the great majority are in the space between £6 and £10. For supermarket wines, I am convinced that this is where the true value lies. It is fun to taste and rave about expensive 'fine' wines – and there are plenty of those this year – but as habitual supermarket wine shoppers always confess to me, the focus is very much on getting the best the tightly squeezed household budget can stretch to.

Among the top-scoring wines, the honours are fairly well spread. Nation by nation, France is a clear first with 13. Nobody else comes close, with Australia, Chile and Germany tying on four apiece and only Italy reaching three. Spain gets two and there are singletons for the rest. Supermarket of the year in these terms goes to Waitrose with nine, including the only top-scoring rosé, and likewise the only fortified wine. But Tesco comes a close second with seven, thanks largely to the brilliant Finest range, which I tasted very late in the day on the tenth anniversary of the original launch back in 2000. Asda comes in a creditable third with six top scores and there are honours too for the Co-op and Sainsbury's, with four, and three apiece from Majestic and M&S.

The diversity of Waitrose's wine range continues to amaze, and they have an excellent website and home-delivery service, endless discounts, and a wonderful range of 'fine' wines. And in spite of the general belief that the stores are more expensive than those of its rivals, wine prices at Waitrose are fully competitive, and they have a terrific range of cheaper bottles.

The Co-op and Asda are both improving fast, Sainsbury's is picking up with innovations like the House range, but Morrisons – wine-wise – still seems stuck among brands and discounting to me, although I have liked the half-price grande marque champagne offers over the year. Tesco marches on. The website and Wine Club are easy to get on with – and I can say exactly same about Marks & Spencer. Booths, the Lancashire chain to which most of us can get access only via mail order, is less cosy to deal with now its online ordering service has been subsumed into the awesome 'everywine' service, but there is still a great range in the stores.

I have tried numerous wines from Aldi and Lidl, but have very little to report. I wonder whether Asda's takeover of no-frills Netto will inject some interest there, but it's too early to speculate.

A last word on alcohol levels and vintages. In the descriptions of the wines I have mentioned these where they are notably high or low. Any wine with 14 or more per cent alcohol by volume, or with less than 12 per cent alcohol by volume, is noted. For readers to whom such information matters, I hope this is of some help.

If no vintage date is appended to the name in the listings, the wine is 'non-vintage', meaning it is a blend of wines made from two or more different harvests. This is quite usual for cheap wines, and little significance need be attached to it except in dry white wines, where the principle of the newer the better usually applies. Most whites are past their freshest within their first year so buying them when they are older, in whole or part, might be a tad risky.

The top-scoring wines of the year

Red wines

Sainsbury's House Côtes du Rhône	Sainsbury's	£3.69
Cuvée de Chasseur 2009	Waitrose	£3.99
The Co-operative Fairtrade Argentine Malbec Reserva 2009	Co-op	£6.49
Extra Special Coonawarra Cabernet Sauvignon 2006	Asda	£6.78
Finest Barbera d'Asti 2007	Tesco	£6.99
Finest Red Burgundy 2008	Tesco	£6.99
La Grille Pinot Noir 2008	Majestic	£6.99
Extra Special Chianti Classico Riserva 2005	Asda	£7.98
Finest Beyers Truter Pinotage 2008	Tesco	£7.99
Finest St Emilion 2008	Tesco	£7.99
Tsantali Organic Cabernet Sauvignon 2006	Waitrose	£8.49
Cono Sur Reserva Merlot 2008	Waitrose	£8.99
Santa Helena Selección del Directorio Pinot Noir 2008	Asda	£9.98
Gulf Station Pinot Noir 2008	Sainsbury's	£9.99
Limited Edition Finest Viña Mara Rioja Gran Reserva 2000	Tesco	£9.99
Finest Gigondas 2007	Tesco	£12.49
Château Belgrave 2006	Co-op	£18.50

Pink wine

Brown Brothers Moscato Rosa 2009	Waitrose	£6.49

White wines

Concha y Toro Late Harvest Sauvignon Blanc 2006 (37.5cl)	Majestic	£5.99
Kendermanns Roter Berg Riesling 2007	Majestic	£5.99
Inycon Growers' Selection Fiano 2009	Waitrose	£6.49
St Mont 2008	Marks & Spencer	£6.49
Tierra y Hombre Sauvignon Blanc 2009	Marks & Spencer	£6.49
Dr L Riesling 2009	Asda	£6.98
Château Roumieu Sauternes 2006 (37.5cl)	Co-op	£6.99
Finest Albariño 2009	Tesco	£6.99
Palataia Pinot Grigio 2009	Marks & Spencer	£6.99
Wente Morning Fog Chardonnay 2008	Waitrose	£7.99
Extra Special Clare Valley Riesling 2008	Asda	£8.18
Reinhartshausen Riesling Kabinett 2007	Co-op	£9.99
Taste the Difference Pouilly Fumé 2009	Sainsbury's	£9.99
The Ned Pinot Grigio 2009	Waitrose	£9.99
Domaine Naudet Sancerre 2009	Waitrose	£12.49

Fortified wine

Sandeman Imperial Tawny Port	Waitrose	£9.65

Sparkling wines

Sainsbury's Blanc de Noirs Champagne Brut	Sainsbury's	£17.29
Extra Special Vintage Champagne Brut 2002	Asda	£19.07

Asda

The wines at Asda continue to amaze me. In spite of the chain's utilitarian image, with the emphasis so much on value, the range of reds, whites, rosés and sparklers is easily as deep and diverse as those of its giant rivals. It's true that the choice varies widely according to the size of the branch you happen to be shopping in, but even the (relatively) small stores I have been visiting in the last year have had a pretty fair selection.

At the 2010 tasting, out of 120 wines I swirled, sniffed and sipped, six have won unhesitating top scores and 17 have scored nine. More than half the wines tasted have made it into this edition, which is a long way above the average.

How do they do it? Much of the credit must go to Philippa Carr, Asda's Wine Selection Manager and a Master of Wine – the qualification that seems to have become a *sine qua non* for those running the licensed side of any major chain's operation. In the last few years Philippa has transformed what was a rather ordinary brand-dominated range into a proper spectrum of all the world's vineyard regions, many represented by newly introduced own-label wines of impressive quality.

Prices, unsurprisingly, are competitive, and Philippa continues to find bargain wines of real quality in spite of punitive taxation (I never tire of reporting that UK wine duty is the highest not just in Europe, but in the Western world) and sterling's long, steep decline against key currencies such as the US and Australian dollars as well as the euro. We might now be in a long, slow recovery period, but the exchange benefits to consumers, if any, cannot be expected to kick in overnight.

There is a decent choice of wines under £4, and some excellent buys below a fiver. But the real excitement at Asda is to be found just a bit higher up the scale, particularly among the 'Extra Special' own labels around £6 to £8.

Online, Asda does not run a dedicated wine service of the kind thoroughly mastered by Tesco, Waitrose and Marks & Spencer, but you can buy some of the wines for home delivery in the same way as any other groceries. The wine promotions are a mystery to me. Besides occasional multibuy deals, there seems no regular programme of discounting. Arguably, prices are so tight that there's no need.

RED WINES

8 **Asda Argentinian Malbec 2009** £4.28
Soft and yielding, unlike most leathery 'entry-level' Mendoza
Malbecs, this has slurpy black fruit and a keen price.

8 **Camden Park Argentinian Malbec 2009** £6.97
Big, muscular, inky, grippy-spicy but friendly oaked fruit bomb
with an apposite illustration of a prize bull on the label.

9 **Vinalba Patagonian Malbec Syrah 2006** £7.62
'Reassuringly competent,' I wrote, mysteriously, in the
note on this dense, delectably poised, mature silky-rich
80/20 blend with 14.5% alcohol.

ARGENTINA

7 **Asda Australian Cabernet Shiraz 2009** £4.28
Straight oaked hedgerow Cabernet with grip but not harsh
is 14% alcohol, and cheap.

10 **Extra Special Coonawarra
Cabernet Sauvignon 2006** £6.78
Dense browning colour, spirity nose, relishable coffee-and-
fruitcake, mature discreetly oaked Coonawarra classic has
lush, slurpy fruit and 14% alcohol.

8 **Extra Special McLaren Vale Shiraz 2008** £8.18
Near-black colour and correspondingly roasted flavours
to this huge oaked winter red with savoury fruit and spicy
middle, with 14.5% alcohol.

AUSTRALIA

8 **Asda Chilean Merlot 2009** £3.28
Simple morello-cherry slurper with buses on the label.

8 **Asda Chilean Cabernet Sauvignon 2009** £3.31
Cheery ripe, well-developed and healthy blackcurrant
bargain; I even like the red pick-up truck label.

CHILE

RED WINES

9   **Casillero del Diablo Carmenère 2009** £7.37
From Concha y Toro's ubiquitous (and regularly discounted) range of varietals I particularly like this toothsome, ripe, pure-fruit-juice bomb from the enigmatic Carmenère grape.

8   **Errazuriz Merlot 2009** £7.98
Stock brand is seriously chewy and long with ripe summer fruit highlights.

8   **Mayu Syrah Reserva 2007** £8.97
Minty perfume draws you into this lush and toasty blackberry food wine with 14% alcohol and a fetching silkiness.

10   **Santa Helena Selección del Directorio Pinot Noir 2008** £9.98
Selected by the Director himself, no less, but ignore the grandiosity and thrill to the sweet, amicable, plump, juicy raspberry-cherry creamy classic flavours of a fabulous wine, with 14.5% alcohol. A thoroughly approachable and seductive Pinot.

8   **Extra Special Côtes du Rhône Villages 2009** £5.11
Big, purple, raisiny young wine will come round nicely.

7   **Red Burgundy Pinot Noir 2008** £5.12
Pale, spare, likeable Cave de Lugny (Mâcon) fresh red with a lemon twist to drink cool.

8   **Kiwi Cuvée Pinot Noir 2008** £6.04
From Corsica, a tilty deep-purple wine with a nice briary whiff and proper earthy-cherry Pinot fruit.

8   **Extra Special Minervois 2008** £6.97
Profound purple Syrah-based pepper-briar Mediterranean red.

CHILE

FRANCE

RED WINES

9 La Vieille Ferme 2009 £7.07

Rather grand Rhône (Côtes du Ventoux) is silky and seductive with red-fruit grip and spice. Made by Perrin family of Châteauneuf fame, and it shows.

**7 La Forge Paul Mas
Cabernet Sauvignon 2009** £7.74

This vin de pays d'Oc pretends to grandeur with its long, dense, toasty-oak style, but it probably needs time.

**9 Château Puicheric Cuvée
Les Clots 2007** £7.97

Endearingly named long, smooth, dark and spicy Minervois, mostly Syrah, with satisfying weight and good balance.

**8 Extra Special Châteauneuf
du Pape 2008** £14.47

Immature but already attractive, a nuanced, complex mélange with cigar-box whiff, plums, blackberries and spice in a rich texture with 14% alcohol.

8 Asda Valpolicella £3.98

Mixed-vintage wine from good Cantina Valpantena is cherry bright but substantial and authentic.

8 Casa Lella Nero d'Avola 2009 £4.98

Indigenous Sicilian has lurid mauve colour, near-jammy ripeness but a nicely balanced mouthfeel with a hint of spicy bitter chocolate and nutskin-dry finish.

9 Extra Special Valpolicella Ripasso 2008 £6.48

I'm a sucker for these reinforced Valpols, including this nicely weighted marzipan-cherry plumpster with its hint of white pepper.

RED WINES

ITALY

9 **Extra Special Barbera D'Asti 2007** £6.98
It's like biting into a giant plum, so juicy and healthily thick-skinned is this bumper purple bouncer, made by respectable Araldica and with a very ripe 14% alcohol and rich oak contact.

8 **Extra Special Primitivo 2007** £6.98
Deep red solid Puglia wine by Girelli of 'Canaletto' fame is rather rich and velvety with a dark heart and a nice tang at the edge.

10 **Extra Special Chianti Classico Riserva 2005** £7.98
There's a lot of Chianti in the supermarkets, much of it good but expensive. This one is cheap for what it is – a deep, de luxe, raspberry-plum, nutty, dry, mature, pure-Sangiovese classically flavoured wine with, weirdly, a screwcap.

N ZEALAND

9 **Extra Special New Zealand Pinot Noir 2008** £9.20
Crisply fresh and bright cherry style, very pale in colour but firm in delicious definition of Pinot fruit, by Wither Hills winery – bit of a bargain, this.

PORTUGAL

9 **Asda Portuguese Red** £3.87
It's partly the price, but this dark charmer with its generous cloves-and-cinnamon-spiced minty-blackberry fruit is thoroughly distinctive and forthcoming. An outstanding anonymous Lisbon-region wine, true to the Portuguese style.

S AFRICA

8 **Hope's Garden Cabernet Sauvignon 2008** £6.41
Blood coloured and splendidly soupy blackberry-and-bitumen wine with vanilla richness and 14.5% alcohol.

RED WINES

9 **Asda Marques del Norte Rioja 2009**   £4.06
Hefty, young-tasting, unoaked, modern, vigorously fruity Rioja of stalwart character and 14% alcohol – and cheap.

8 **The Pilgrimage Mazuelo 2008**   £7.07
Intense purple cherry-prune oaked Extramadura red with long, clean-edged fruit and 14% alcohol.

9 **Castillo de Albai Reserva 2005**   £8.72
A pure Tempranillo 'exclusively from the best plots located in La Rioja Alta', it's grand stuff with a sweet vanilla nose and smooth, rounded and beguiling black fruit.

8 **Ravenswood Zinfandel
Vintners Blend 2007**   £7.48
Easy-to-like liquorice and sweet black cherry smoothie.

PINK WINES

9 **Santa Helena Solar Rosé 2009**   £6.14
Coral colour to this pure Cabernet Sauvignon with firm, crisp expressive flavour; defined, refreshing, delicious.

8 **Extra Special Chilean
Shiraz Rosé 2009**   £6.27
Lurid intense colour, assertive summer-pudding fruit including apple, but brisk and crunchy. A big food wine, recognisably Shiraz.

8 **Extra Special Languedoc Rosé 2009**   £6.37
Delicately pale colour but a forcefully strawberry-sweet aroma, then crisp dry freshness. Likeable Syrah-based Mediterranean pink.

SPAIN

USA

CHILE

FRANCE

PINK WINES

8 Pleyades Garnacha Rosada 2009 £5.16
This Carinena rosé has it all: gaudy label, bright shocking-pink colour, bubblegum nose, healthy spare briar fruit; good food wine.

8 Murviedro Rosé 2009 £5.98
Magenta wine from Valencia tastes as its Garnacha-Cabernet blend should, with crunchy freshness and dry finish.

WHITE WINES

8 Asda Argentinian Torrontes 2009 £4.47
Friendly, exotic, Muscat-like dry indigenous white with a nutty finish. Do try it as an aperitif.

9 Extra Special Adelaide Hills
Chardonnay 2008 £7.98
Gold, rich, old-fashioned, buttered-toast and apple-pie oaked Chardy with 14% alcohol retains stony freshness and even elegance. It grows on you.

10 Extra Special Clare Valley
Riesling 2008 £8.18
This is the same wine that scored 10/10 in last year's edition: 'succulent, powerful Riesling constructed on the nectarine model...', but inexplicably it hasn't sold out. Age has not wearied its appeal, so buy now.

8 Zilzie Viognier 2009 £8.18
People must be drinking Viognier if supermarkets keep stocking it, but it's mostly rubbish; this yellow, exotic, near-oxidised marzipan-and-apricot variation is well above the average.

7 Chilean Chardonnay 2009   £3.38
Peary but respectable unoaked clean bargain.

**9 Extra Special Chilean
Sauvignon Blanc 2009**   £6.27
A jolly giant by Errazuriz featuring asparagus, grass and
nettles and providing ample refreshment and stimulation
at modest expense.

8 Palo Alto Sauvignon Blanc 2009   £7.81
Popular brand is grassy, tangy and lively with a lemon rim
– convincing competition for the Kiwi market leaders.

8 Errazuriz Chardonnay 2009   £8.07
Rich, ripe opening flavour, closing citrus-brisk with
coconutty oak influence in between. Fun.

9 Asda Vin de Pays d'Oc Marsanne 2009   £3.98
Understated, beautifully balanced, fresh dry white evoking
blanched almonds and citrus fruit, all at a bargain price.

**8 Château Salmonière Muscadet de Sèvre
et Maine Sur Lie 2009**   £6.07
Authentic briny Loire white with plenty of grass and tang.
The definitive match for moules marinières.

9 Asda Petit Chablis 2007   £7.07
Proper gold-coloured gunflint Chablis abounding with
lush Chardonnay fruit and just 11.5% alcohol.

8 Extra Special Gewürztraminer 2008   £7.07
Big ripe Alsace wine with trademark lychee nose and
exotic fruit.

8 Extra Special Chablis 2008   £8.97
Mineral, tangy style is bracing and stimulating. For adults,
from respected Jean Marc Brocard.

10 Dr L Riesling 2009   £6.98
Flagbearer for pure Moselle Riesling is apple-crisp, nearly spritzy, so mineral and racy and uniquely stimulating, and just 8.5% alcohol. Why isn't this the bestselling white wine in Britain?

8 Asda Soave 2009   £3.28
Easy-drinking, extremely cheap but genuine Soave is bright, fresh and crisp, and 11.5% alcohol.

9 Casa Lella Cataratto 2009   £4.98
Interesting herbaceous, nutty aromatic Sicilian dry-but-rich, lemon-edged wine to match cured meats, creamy pasta dishes and fish.

9 Extra Special Fiano 2009   £5.98
From Sicilian jumbo-co-op Settesoli, a fine lemon-gold, sweetly aromatic orchard-almond dry white of great character.

8 Extra Special Pinot Grigio 2009   £6.08
Made by distinguished Trentino outfit Alois Lageder, a brightly fresh and attractively exotic variation on the eternal theme.

8 Church Mouse Falanghina 2009   £6.98
Mystifying name, but there is much to intrigue in the depth and savour of this long-flavoured, grassy-lush Puglian food wine. Fish and poultry.

8 Extra Special Gavi 2009   £7.24
Flavour starts pleasingly green, then turns lush and dimensional in that nutty-brassica way of Gavi. Interesting and likeable.

8 **Montana Sauvignon Blanc**
Reserve 2009 £8.98

Big-brand Kiwi is as generously expressive as ever with its vivid nettles-and-grass zingy lushness and long, long flavours.

8 **Fairhills Rawsonville Chenin**
Chardonnay 2009 £5.44

Seductive honey whiff from this crowd-pleasing oaked blend made by 'the largest Fairtrade project in the world'.

8 **Asda Moscatel de Valencia** £3.58

For sweet-wine lovers, a real treat: yellow colour, ambrosial grapy richness, easy weight and 15% alcohol.

8 **Torres Viña Sol 2009** £5.97

Another bright and zesty vintage from the ubiquitous and consistent Penedès brand; good value, even without the frequent discounting.

10 **Extra Special Vintage**
Champagne Brut 2002 £19.07

Still on sale, I ranked this 10/10 last year and it's every bit as good on retasting – gold colour, generous toasty flavours mellowed with maturity, and the price is lower than before, in spite of big duty increases.

9 **Asda Rosé Champagne** £19.12

Onion-skin colour and billowing strawberry nose are followed up by the most enticing and vivid flavours with creamy richness but crisp finish. Outstandingly good, and it actually tastes pink.

8 **Dubois Caron Champagne** £24.21

New one to me, with lemony twang finishing extravagant yeasty fruit. Look out for this one on discount.

Asda Asti £4.78

Very pale and sweet, short of sticky, gently foaming, and 7.5% alcohol.

 Asda Cava Demi Sec £4.26

Soft rather than sweet, a rather charming contrivance with lively mousse, balancing acidity and 11.5% alcohol.

Booths

This family-owned company, founded in 1847, well before any of the better-known chains, has just 26 supermarkets, all in the north-west of England. The company is much admired in its own region, and from afar by southerners like me for its impeccably chosen wine range which is, thank goodness, available in its entirety online. The store range of 600-or-so different wines is incorporated into Booths' mammoth web operation **www.everywine.co.uk**, a service offering a vast number of wines (more than 38,000 of them last time I looked), by the case. For the less-daunting task of shopping online at Booths, so to speak, you simply go to the site, click on the 'mix your own case' icon and take it from there.

Based on my own experience, delivery is very prompt and the charge is £5.95 whatever the size of your order (including a single bottle), and wherever you live on the mainland.

RED WINES

AUSTRALIA

 8 **Peter Lehman Clancy's**
Shiraz-Cabernet-Merlot 2007 £7.89
Big spicy Barossa fruit bomb with 14.5% alcohol is really
quite poised and refined – but I continue to detect a pleasingly
yeoman hint of Daddies Sauce somewhere in there.

 8 **Chat en Oeuf 2007** £4.99
Yes, the name is a silly jape, complete with a cat and an egg
on the label, but this Côtes du Ventoux Grenache-Syrah
parody of grandiose neighbour Châteauneuf du Pape is
really rather good, especially in the great southern Rhône
vintage of 2007.

FRANCE

 8 **Beaujolais Bully 2009** £5.99
This wildly juicy but grippy raspberry refresher from the
fabled 2009 harvest should have replaced the less exciting
2008 by now.

8 **L'Olivier de la Rèze Minervois 2005** £5.99
On the off-chance that there's any left, do try this organically
made Syrah-based spicy Mediterranean gripper in its ripe
maturity.

 9 **Château Ducla 2005** £6.99
I visited this Graves (Bordeaux) property in 2006 and
tasted the 2005 vintage, mostly Merlot, from the vat; it's
turned out deliciously keen and ripe and healthy, now
plumply mature.

 8 **St Joseph Cave St Désirat 2006** £8.99
Silky northern Rhône Syrah is benefiting from time in
bottle, spicy and rich with blackberry fruit.

RED WINES

ITALY

9   **Cantine Due Palme Tenuta Al Sole 2006**   £5.49
There's still some of this dark briar Salento Negroamaro
left over from last year – a lovely mature bargain.

8   **Cantina Valpantena Falasco**
Ripasso Valpolicella 2007   £8.29
One of the best of these reinforced Veneto reds I've tasted,
this is dark, nutty and dense with rich-cherry fruit, but
finishes very dry and brisk.

SPAIN

8   **Gran Tesoro Garnacha 2009**   £3.99
Juicy and plump midweight party red from Campo de Borja
(south of Rioja) has a spicy twist and gives good value.

8   **Bodegas Ochoa Tempranillo**
Garnacha 2008   £6.99
From the grape-mix that dominates in next-door Rioja,
this muscular, minty-spicy Navarra is a red very much in
its own style – dark, brooding, very satisfying.

8   **Capçanes Mas Collet 2007**   £7.99
Spicy, minty, sweetly ripe black fruit Catalan red of
muscular intensity.

WHITE WINES

AUSTRALIA

9   **Brown Brothers Dry**
Muscat Blanc 2008   £5.79
Perennially among Australia's quirkiest and best-value wines,
the aromas and flavours of this honeyed but fresh fruit basket
encompass pineapple, ginger, lychee and nectarine.

9 Premières Côtes de Bordeaux £5.69

Yvon Mau, a very good Bordeaux producer, is at last putting the words 'Sweet White Wine' on the label of this gloriously rich but beautifully balanced 'dessert' nectar. At the price an absolute gift to the sweet-toothed – and that includes me.

8 Cave de Lugny Chardonnay 2008 £5.99

Steely but generous Mâconnais with apple crispness and a lick of sweet melon.

9 Gau Bickelheimer Kürfurstenstück Auslese 2008 £5.49

Gift of wine from the Rheinhessen is gold, honeyed and balanced with 10% alcohol. Muller-Thürgau rather than Riesling, which helps to explain the very low price.

8 Louis Guntrum Riesling 2008 £5.99

Delicate sweet-apple but crisply balanced Rhine QbA of real charm.

8 Villa Wolf Pinot Gris 2008 £6.99

Deliciously aromatic and smoky Rhine curiosity in a posh, burgundy-style bottle is dry but pungent and exotic. Made by the great Ernst Loosen.

8 Wither Hills Sauvignon Blanc 2009 £8.99

Noticeably full, ripe gooseberry fruit with a suggestion of sherbet in this long, lavish but tangy food wine – try it with oysters.

8 Torres Viña Esmeralda 2009 £7.69

Mostly Muscat, but dry with aromas of honey, lychees and sweet table grapes, a delightfully fresh and exotic aperitif wine from near Barcelona.

PORTUGAL

9 Blandy's Duke of Clarence
Rich Madeira £12.39
This is fabulous, just one of half a dozen great Blandy Madeiras now becoming deservedly well known. Clarence is a nutty-gold colour with intoxicating figgy, toasted aromas and a rich, soothing marzipan fruit, short of sweet but memorably luscious. Chill it for aperitif drinking.

SPAIN

8 Booths Manzanilla £5.69
Particularly tangy and fresh pale bone-dry sherry by top Sanlucar outfit Hidalgo is 15% alcohol and good value.

8 Cave de Lugny Sparkling Burgundy £7.99
Excellent Chardonnay fizz from a good Mâconnais outfit with nice yeasty-almondy richness as well as crunchy apple freshness. Usually known as Crémant de Bourgogne, the anglicised name might help put it on the map.

FRANCE

9 H Blin Champagne Brut 2002 £22.99
Still here, maturing nicely, a gorgeous biscuity vintage bubbly at £1 cheaper than it was in last year's edition.

9 Medici Concerto Lambrusco 2007 £8.99
Bravo, Booths, for persisting with this fabulous authentic, gently foaming, dry summer-fruit refresher, keeping the proud name of true Lambrusco alive.

ITALY

Co-op

The Co-operative Explorer's Vineyard Sauvignon Blanc 2009, a New Zealand wine I hugely admire, is on sale at 3,304 of the Co-op's sprawling empire of outlets throughout the country. I can buy it in the small but well-stocked branch in my own town, Castle Cary (pop. 2,096) in Somerset, and have done so on more than one occasion. On the other hand, Reinhartshausen Riesling Kabinett 2007, a Rheingau, Germany, wine I also esteem greatly, is on sale at only 300 Co-op shops. Castle Cary doesn't have it, nor does it have most of the wines mentioned in this section, which have very varied levels of distribution across the network.

I mention this because I am well aware how annoying it is to follow up a recommendation, get to the store and find the staff have never heard of it. It's a problem common to all the retail grocery chains, but the Co-op is easily the worst offender. It does, after all, have by far the largest number of stores – lately boosted by the absorption of 800 former Somerfield supermarkets – and, paradoxically, the least number of different wines of any of the big players.

All that said, the Co-op offers lots of great buys, regular discounts, and easily the best range of Fairtrade wines anywhere. And given the enormity of the operation, there is probably a really big Co-op with most, if not all, of the wine range, somewhere quite near where you live.

RED WINES

8 Las Moras Bonarda 2009   £5.25

Rangy slick blackberry fruit in this rugged Andean red – muscular but poised.

**10 The Co-operative Fairtrade
Argentine Malbec Reserva 2009**   £6.49

Icon wine – it's the best Fairtrade product I've tasted all year, dense purple in colour with an alluring toasty blackberry-pie aroma and corresponding rich, brambly flavours with a distinct bitter-chocolate note at the heart of the flavour and a dry, even tangy, Italian-style finish.

**9 The Co-operative Bin 99 Argentine
Cabernet Franc Reserve 2007**   £6.99

Ambitious oaked wine from the grape that makes Loire Valley reds shows recognisable green stalky character, and very nice too; a fine, edgy, but generously ripe 14% alcohol red-meat partner.

**8 The Co-operative Mendoza
Malbec 2008**   £7.99

Hearty (14% alcohol) carnivore's red has leather and spearmint on the nose and pruny topnote to the dark berry fruit.

**8 Nepenthe Charleston
Pinot Noir 2007**   £10.99

Plenty of deep ruby colour and a lot of well-defined earthy-pure cherry-raspberry Pinot fruit. Look out for discounts.

8 Santa Rita Carmenère 2008   £6.99

Fine carmine colour (that's how the Carmenère grape gets its name) and sleek ripe fruit in this distinctive oaked wine.

8 Maycas del Limari Syrah 2008   £8.99

Nice soft-tannic grip at the finish and ripe fruit makes you think of biting into a Victoria plum, but with strong, dark blackberry fruit with toffee highlights; 14.5% alcohol.

ARGENTINA

AUSTRALIA

CHILE

RED WINES

FRANCE

9 Château L'Estang 2007 £8.99
Unexpectedly gracious and elegant claret from the Côtes de Castillon, which isn't renowned as Bordeaux's most beguiling appellation; slinky and rounded and good value.

8 Perrin Côtes du Rhône Nature 2009 £8.99
Bright mauve organic spicy red with 14.5% alcohol needed time to round out when I tasted it, but there were prospects of real interest.

10 Château Belgrave 2006 £18.50
A grand cru classé of the Médoc (Bordeaux) of quite wonderful quality, dark, sleek and cedary, plummy and already drinking very well, although it will develop for at least five more years. One of the Co-op's 'Fine Wines', so sold only in the 300 biggest outlets.

ITALY

9 Moramari Salice Salentino 2008 £4.99
Dark volcanic spicy Negroamaro from Puglia is impressively rich and supple, especially for the money.

8 Casa Contini Brindisi Riserva 2006 £5.99
Beguiling redcurrant fruit in this mature Puglian pasta-matcher.

9 Ricossa Barbera D'Asti 2007 £5.99
Immediately appealing juicy brambly and eager refreshing oaked wine has 14% alcohol but a light touch.

N ZEALAND

8 Marlborough Estate Reserve Merlot 2009 £6.99
Leafy-black-cherry nose on a rather lush and mellow midweight Merlot.

PORTUGAL

9 Ramada Tinto 2007 £3.99
This bargain brand is improving, better integrated than of old with a nice clove spice to the black, minty fruit.

RED WINES

PORTUGAL

🍷 8 **Star Mountain**
Shiraz-Aragonês-Trincadeira 2008   £4.99
Dense and tannic with appreciable oak presence, this delivers a lot of tastebud-gripping blackcurrant ripeness for the money. Distinctly Portuguese, and distinctly enjoyable.

SPAIN

🍷 9 **Corte Mayor Rioja Crianza 2005**   £8.99
Retro-labelled sweetly ripe vanilla-rich pure-Tempranillo wine has juicy bounce as well as mellow maturity and elegant weight.

PINK WINES

FRANCE

🍷 9 **Les Crouzes Cinsault Rosé 2009**   £4.99
Cracking dry crisp Mediterranean pink is so fresh it quenches thirst.

🍷 8 **The Frenchhouse Rosé 2009**   £5.29
Coral-coloured dry summer soft fruit style with a lick of sweetness; a crowd-pleaser.

SPAIN

🍷 8 **Tocado Rosado 2009**   £4.99
From Campo de Borja, south of Rioja, this magenta Garnacha-Merlot blend is ripe but crisp and properly pink-flavoured.

USA

🍷 7 **Crow's Landing Shiraz-Cabernet**
Rosé 2009   £4.99
Quite sweet, but not cloying, a commercial brand with redeeming summer fruitiness.

WHITE WINES

AUSTRALIA

🍷 8 **McGuigan Classic**
Sauvignon Blanc 2010   £6.99
Long gooseberry fruit in a brisk, business-like medium with just 11% alcohol.

BULGARIA

🍷**7** The Co-operative Bulgarian
Chardonnay 2009 £3.99

Throwback wine (remember the 1980s?) is attractively presented, softly ripe and endearing.

CHILE

🍷**8** The Co-operative Chilean
Chardonnay 2009 £3.99

Good straight snappy-apple, hint-of-peach ripe and dry style.

🍷**8** The Co-operative Leyda Valley
Sauvignon Blanc 2009 £7.99

Bristling nettly bold fresh and decidely assertive aperitif wine with 14% alcohol.

FRANCE

🍷**9** Monbazillac Domaine du
Haut-Rauly 2005 37.5cl £5.99

Lovely toffee and lemon balance in this gloriously honeyed pure-Semillon pud wine.

🍷**10** Château Roumieu Sauternes 2006 37.5cl £6.99

I am repeating this from last year's edition because my mole at the Co-op whispers that they still have some left and it could appear anytime at a promotional price of £6.99 (supposedly halved). To reiterate: 'Ambrosial ... Succulent, honeyed ... Fleetingly limey.'

🍷**8** The Co-operative Chablis 2008 £8.99

It does have the keen gunflint minerality you hope for in proper Chablis – classic unoaked Chardonnay made by commendable Brocard estate.

GERMANY

🍷**10** Reinhartshausen Riesling
Kabinett 2007 £9.99

I was agog to find this brilliant wine at the tasting: gold colour, lush sweet apple style more at the Spätlese level than Kabinett (I thought) and an absolute classic racy Riesling character, with 9.5% alcohol. As one of the Co-op's new 20-strong list of 'Fine Wines' it is sold only in the biggest 300 stores.

NEW ZEALAND

🍷8 **Azure Estate Sauvignon 2009** £6.25
Economy wine has asparagus whiff and quite austere fruit, and refreshes nicely.

🍷8 **The Co-operative Explorer's
Vineyard Unoaked Chardonnay 2009** £7.49
Heaps of crisp apple in this pebbly-dry but luxuriant balanced wine in the pure-fruit Kiwi tradition.

🍷9 **The Co-operative Explorer's
Vineyard Sauvignon Blanc 2009** £7.99
Gooseberry fruit with nettly follow-up in a long, clean and classy flavour trail; super wine at a pretty good price.

S.AFRICA

🍷8 **The Co-operative Fairtrade Cape
Sauvignon Blanc Reserve 2009** £6.79
Crisply grassy and fresh, bright with gooseberry zest and yet substantial and long in its fruitiness and weight.

USA

🍷7 **Six Mile Road Symphony 2008** £4.99
Symphony is a grape-cross from Grenache and Muscat and this tastes likes a dry(ish) Muscat. Try very chilled as an aperitif.

FRANCE

🍷8 **The Co-operative Sparkling Saumur** £8.49
Good to see this esoteric Loire sparkler with hearty orchard fruit and a crisp dry edge. Only in superstores.

🍷9 **Les Pionniers Champagne Brut** £16.40
Rich colour, baked apple nose and long, full, autumn-fruit flavours make this a very appealing fizz. Don't be put off by the odd name.

ITALY

🍷8 **The Co-operative Prosecco** £7.99
Nicely packaged pear-juice, not-too-sweet, fresh and lively style with 11% alcohol.

Majestic

Majestic's prices are a minefield for a reporter like me. All the figures listed in the following pages were correct when this book was in preparation, but take them with a pinch of salt. The chances are that most of them are way above what you will actually be asked to pay. Majestic's perpetual discounts, based on the multibuy principle of buy two bottles get 20 per cent or more off, cover a large proportion of the list at any one time, and regularly operate on a region- or nation-of-origin basis – buy any two wines from the Languedoc, Australia or Spain or wherever and get 20 per cent off.

Given that there is a minimum purchase at Majestic, buying two bottles of the same wine is hardly a problem. And in case you haven't heard, that minimum is now six bottles rather than the dozen with which the company persisted for its first 30 years or so, bringing in the change in time for the recession-bruised Christmas of 2009. Majestic profits have continued to burgeon ever since.

Asked by The Sunday Times to account for the extraordinary success of his business, Majestic's managing director Steve Lewis replied that he likes to 'wake up every morning and work out what the boss of every big supermarket really doesn't want Majestic to do – then do it'.

I fully acknowledge that Majestic is not a supermarket, but in a guide like this, I cannot omit it. The range of wines is bigger than any of the supermarkets' and there is no padding with indifferent brands. There are fine wines, all the way up to classed growth clarets, of a kind unknown to supermarket lists. The advice from staff is generally excellent, and well qualified.

The network of branches now numbers 153 but to buy the wines you need not even stir. Three or four times a year there is a new, comprehensive price list which you can peruse at home, then simply phone your nearest branch and order for delivery at no extra charge for a dozen or more bottles. If you prefer to order online, www.majestic.co.uk is one of the most user-friendly websites of them all.

RED WINES

9 Yalumba Bush Vine Grenache 2008 £9.49
Toasty, toffee-hinting, poised, yummy-fruit Barossa easy-drinker with long spiced flavours and 14.5% alcohol.

8 Jim Barry The Lodge Hill Shiraz 2007 £9.99
Deep maroon Clare Valley blackberry monster with 14.5% alcohol is very well balanced.

9 D'Arenberg Dead Arm Shiraz 2006 £25.00
Famous McLaren Vale wine is thrillingly long and lush with what I cannot resist calling a firm grip, and 15% alcohol. Is it worth the astronomical price? Yes.

AUSTRALIA

8 Adobe Merlot 2008 £7.49
Well-focused chocolate-and-cherry organic tightly finishing balanced wine.

**8 De Martino 347 Vineyards
Carmenère Reserva 2008** £7.49
Blueberry fruit with a tangy edge forms the core of this tastebud-grabber – good sticky-pasta-matcher.

**9 Novas Winemaker's Selection
Syrah 2007** £12.49
Exciting, silky, bright-fruit green-edged style to an organic 14.5% alcohol wine I felt was what Crozes-Hermitage aspires to be, but rarely is. Really like this.

CHILE

**8 Alain Grignon Carignan
Vieilles Vignes 2009** £6.99
Eager young Hérault picnic red is light in colour and weight, with endearing sunny fruitiness.

**8 Domaine Sainte Rose La Garrigue
Syrah Grenache 2007** £6.99
Spicy smooth black fruit middleweight (though with 14% alcohol) does have some of the thyme and rosemary flavour elements associated with the Garrigue.

FRANCE

RED WINES

FRANCE

10 La Grille Pinot Noir 2008   £6.99
Worthy successor to the 2007 top-scorer from St-Pourçain
in the Loire, this is pale, cool and elegant with a leafy-
green freshness highlighting the pure, poised raspberry
silky fruit; a distinctive style that is such good value – try
it cool with chicken dishes.

8 Vallée Blanche Malbec 2009   £6.99
Languedoc wine reminiscent of the leathery Argentine
style turns out to have a lot of juicy cassis fruit. Friendly.

**8 Plan de Dieu Côtes du Rhône
Villages 2007**   £7.99
Snap these 2007 CdRs up while they last – this one has a
nice green-pepper note to the spicy red-fruit aroma and
flavour, and 14% alcohol.

**9 Beaujolais Villages
Château de Terrière 2009**   £8.99
There's hope for Beaujolais yet as this spiffing purple
sparky rhubarb and raspberry bouncer from the vaunted
2009 harvest (best vintage since 1978, I've heard) amply
demonstrates. Lovely juicy wine.

8 Morgon Château de Pizay 2009   £8.99
Remarkably dense purply-black and gripping, quite
weighty but typically juicy Gamay fruit in this serious
Beaujolais. It will evolve for a year or two.

**9 Bourgueil Les Cent Boisselées
Pierre-Jacques Druet 2003**   £9.99
Where else would you find wine like this? A mature Loire
classic with browning colour, delicious mellow coffee-and-
prune Cabernet Franc fruit full of lipsmacking life.

RED WINES

8 Château du Haut-Plateau 2007   **£9.99**
Firm and robust Montagne-St-Emilion (Bordeaux) has
hallmark cedar notes and long, slinky, Merlot-dominated
black fruit. Good now and will develop.

9 Château St-Colombe 2004   **£9.99**
Nicely mature Côtes de Castillon (Bordeaux) has a very
expensive aroma and long, sleek artful toasty-oak fruit
flavours. Posh claret at a good price.

**8 Saumur Champigny
Château de Targé 2007**   **£9.99**
Richly ripe and dark leafy-fresh Loire Cabernet Franc is
substantial and delivers a real rush of purply flavours.

8 Château Grivière 2001   **£11.99**
A Médoc (Bordeaux) cru bourgeois with a proper enticing
'old claret' nose and poised, sleek fruit.

8 Volnay Labouré Roi 2006   **£11.99**
Bright, earthy, authentic red burgundy from a big negoçiant
is a treat – you don't see much Volnay at this price.

8 Beaune 1er Cru Louis Jadot 2005   **£19.99**
Big-name, big-price burgundy from an exceptional vintage
is still vigorously fruity and tannic with a lively citrus edge.
Safe buy for a special occasion.

9 I Monili Primitivo del Tarantino 2009   **£6.24**
Easy-drinking Puglian juicy black fruit wine has refreshing
new-squished fruit flavours and artful balance, finishing
ideally dry.

8 Polago Vallesanta 2008   **£7.49**
Intense briary Umbrian red, largely from the Sangiovese
grape of Chianti, is juicily fruity and balanced.

RED WINES

ITALY

8 **I Satiri Salice Salentino Riserva 2005** £8.49
Colour is browning in this splendid old dark, even burnt, heel-of-Italy brimstone red with roasty oak and a great dry nutskin finish.

9 **La Casetta di Ettore Righetti Valpolicella Classico Superiore Ripasso 2006** £14.99
I have admired this sumptuous Verona rarity for years, progessively despairing at its escalting price, but it is superb – dark and silky, plumply supple and youthful even at this age, and no doubt immortal.

N ZEALAND

8 **Craggy Range Te Kahu 2009** £13.74
Big minty Merlot-Cabernets blend from Gimblett Gravels, Hawke's Bay, is rich, slick and satisfying.

S AFRICA

8 **Kanonkop Pinotage 2007** £16.99
Famed Stellenbosch indigenous wine has a typical tarmac whiff, rich new-oak smoothness, but well-defined hedgerow-fruit flavours and 14% alcohol; a worthy flag-flyer for the Cape.

SPAIN

8 **Berberana Classico 1877 Reserva 2005** £7.99
From the DO of Mentrida near Madrid, this is a sweetly oaked, plausible (but not unconvincing) long-aged bargain in the Rioja style.

8 **Priorat Mas de Subira 2006** £12.99
Emerging Catalan cult region is well represented by this dense ritzy red spiced with cloves, truffles and mint at what is a relatively modest price for Priorat. Reminds me of good Vino Nobile di Montepulciano and has 14.5% alcohol.

RED WINES

USA

8 **Robert Mondavi Pinot Noir 2008** £14.99
Intense earthy-raspberry creamy-oaked slinky classic with
scary but undetectable 15.5% alcohol needs to have the
£5 discount that applied when I tasted it.

PINK WINES

CHILE

8 **Viña Leyda Costero**
Pinot Noir Rosé 2009 £8.69
Colour is close to red, but it tastes convincingly pink, with
ripe but fresh and dry raspberry flavours edged with a
distinct grapefruit acidity.

FRANCE

9 **La Grille Pinot Noir Rosé 2009** £6.99
Salmon colour, whiff of summer pudding and fresh keen
flavour in this delightful Loire pink.

8 **Commanderie de Payrassol Rosé 2009** £9.99
Dry but not austere Côtes de Provence with firm strawberry
element and a nice balance of fruit and freshness. Elegant.

ITALY

7 **Cavalchina Estate Bardolino**
Chiaretto 2009 £8.74
Coral-coloured, soft cherry-fruit pink is borderline sweet
and rather expensive at full price.

SPAIN

8 **Muga Rioja Rosado 2009** £8.99
Nice bold crunchy red fruit finishing dry, made with a mix
of black Garnacha and Tempranillo and Viura.

8 **Peter Lehmann Riesling 2008** £8.69
Don't let the naff nymphet label put you off this fine, bracing, limey food wine – rice dishes and fish.

8 **Kangarilla Road Chardonnay 2009** £10.99
McLaren Vale perennial is reliably ripe, toasty and alive with sweet-apple fruit. Price is escalating, though.

10 **Concha y Toro Late Harvest**
Sauvignon Blanc 2006 37.5cl £5.99
During these terrible economic times in Broken Britain, we all need to spend more time at home with a wine like this. It is a sublime honeyed pud wine to sip very chilled as an aid to contemplation of the resourcefulness of mankind and the marriage of agriculture and artistry that creates a wine like this at a price ordinary mortals can afford.

8 **Adobe Chardonnay 2009** £7.49
Big crunchy apple organic wine with 14% alcohol.

8 **Viña Leyda Costero Riesling 2009** £8.74
Nicely extracted limey dry Riesling in the Aussie manner (as distinct from German) has brisk apple fruit.

8 **Winemaker's Lot Viognier**
Lo Ovalle Vineyard 2009 £9.49
Insinuating mellow apricot fruit is nicely balanced with a keen citrus acidity; 14% alcohol.

8 **Errazuriz Wild Ferment**
Chardonnay 2008 £10.99
I suppose this wine is a bit obvious, with its rich peachy fruit, lush creamy texture and heady 14% alcohol, but I like it just the same, and admire the brave use of wild rather than cultured yeasts.

FRANCE

**9 Domaine de la Tourmaline Muscadet
de Sèvre et Maine Sur Lie 2009** £6.99
Top example of the briny Loire mussel-matcher is bone-dry
but racing with grassy-lush fruit. Hearty and substantial.

**8 Domaine Ste Rose Le Vent
du Nord 2008** £6.99
Attractive mélange from Roussanne and Chardonnay in
the vin de pays d'Oc has creamy oak and lemon tang –
good food white.

**8 La Grille Cool-Fermented
Chenin Blanc 2009** £6.99
Sherbet, honey and tangy lime are all to be found in this
charming Loire dry white with just 11% alcohol.

**9 La Grille Touraine
Sauvignon Blanc 2009** £6.99
Limey twang finishes this lovely vivid Loire refresher.

8 Sancerre Les Baudières 2009 £10.99
Meadow fruit and freshness in this pebble-dry but
intriguingly complex classic Loire Sauvignon.

**8 Mâcon-Milly-Lamartine
Clos du Four 2009** £11.99
From Majestic's darling burgundy dealer Christophe
Cordier, a yellow, buttery classic Chardonnay with nice
citrus balance.

**8 Beaune Blanc 1er Cru du Château,
Bouchard Père et Fils, 2006** £19.99
Textbook white burgundy is lush with mineral Chardonnay
fruit, rich with toasty, creamy oak contact and from a
good, maturing vintage. Safe bet.

10 Kendermanns Roter Berg Riesling 2007 £5.99
From the people who make Black Tower, a simply fabulous
stony, crisp and exuberantly ripe and stimulating dry wine of
huge charm from the Rheinpfalz just across the border from
Alsace. It stuck out a mile, and is terrific value. On the day it
was on offer at £2 off for two bottles – £3.99 apiece.

8 Sistina Pecorino 2009 £8.74
From the Marches, Italy's Midlands, a characterful green-
fruit, grassy and healthy dry white from the Pecorino
grape. Deserves to be better known.

8 Falanghina Terredora 2009 £9.99
Bracing Campania dry wine with a crafty balance of
blanched-almond richness and twangy lemon acidity
– ideal match for creamy pasta dishes and risottos as well
as fish and poultry.

8 Fairhall Cliffs Sauvignon Blanc 2009 £6.24
Bold green glittery Marlborough wine is cheap, at no cost
to intensity or interest.

9 Waimea Estate Gewürztraminer 2009 £11.99
Whopping lychee-scented heavyweight with 14% alcohol
is in the Alsace vendange tardive style at a fraction of the
price, and the balance is perfect – trimmed with a super
grapefruit acidity.

8 The Ned Noble
   Sauvignon Blanc 2009 37.5cl £12.49
In an unstable tall and narrow bottle, a gently sweet
'dessert' wine probably better treated as an aperitif, with a
light touch, and an unbeatable name.

8 Saint Clair Pioneer Block 19
   Bird Block Sauvignon Blanc 2009 £14.99
Premium single-vineyard Marlborough wine is worth
paying for because it has arresting concentration and
breadth of fruit.

GERMANY

ITALY

NEW ZEALAND

NEW ZEALAND

♆ 9 **Saint Clair Pioneer Block 10**
Twin Hills Chardonnay 2008 £14.99
Love this plush but pebbly creamy-coconut oaked mineral
balanced Marlborough Chardy with 14% alcohol. A Kiwi
wine through and through, and there's nothing else like it.

♆ 8 **Cape Crest Sauvignon Blanc 2008** £17.49
By Te Mata of Hawke's Bay, a lovely lush and long
Sauvignon-Semillon blend in which new oak works its
magic. An experience.

SPAIN

♆ 8 **Marqués de Riscal Rueda Blanco 2009** £7.99
Famous Rioja name has branched out successfully with
this seaside fresh and boldly fruity Verdejo.

♆ 9 **Vega de la Reina Verdejo 2008** £7.99
Super-fresh green-grass Verdejo-Sauvignon blend from
Rueda with full, assertive crisp orchard fruit. Makes a big
impression.

CHILE

♆ 8 **Casillero del Diablo Brut**
Reserva Chardonnay 2008 £5.99
Overt Chardonnay fruit in this brightly flavoured party fizz.

N ZEALAND

♆ 8 **Cloudy Bay Pelorus** £19.99
Bracing prestige Kiwi fizz is 80/20 Chardonnay/Pinot Noir
and a legitimate alternative to champagne, though with
little price edge.

Marks & Spencer

 The M&S wine list is an epic. There are 35 different champagnes, few of which you are likely to find anywhere else. There are more than 20 wines from Argentina, and I stopped counting the Italian wines when I went past 50. Australia and New Zealand account for 100. And these are all wines unique to M&S.

Andrew Bird, manager of the wine department, is proud to be different. 'We're determined,' he says, 'to ensure our customers have a great alternative to the ubiquitous brands dominating the ranges of our competitors. M&S is determined to stay true to its principles of quality, value and choice by bringing you new, exclusive wines every year and taking more than a few risks along the way.'

The risks he speaks of are no doubt the one-off wines that so liberally decorate this enormous range. Examples are the intensely likeable Barolo-alternative Renato Ratti Nebbiolo Langhe (an irresistible name, surely), a gorgeous Gascon dry white St Mont from the esoteric Gros Manseng grape, and the best Pinot Grigio in Britain, Palataia, which is made in Germany by former M&S wine staffer Gerd Stepp. If wines like these were not marketed by M&S, I doubt very much that they would appear anywhere else in the mass-retail sector.

I fervently hope that they are all selling well, because they add significantly to the sum of human happiness. Mind you, the quirkier the wine, the less likely you are to find it in any but the biggest stores. But do remember the website at www. marksandspencer.com. I have used this with great success, and it seems to have not only all the wines on the store list, but a great many 'online exclusives' as well – some of which I've reviewed in the following pages.

A further attraction of the site is that it regularly offers huge discounts, sometimes just on particular wines, or on all the wines from a particular nation. And quite often, for a week or two at a time, there is a blanket 25 per cent off the entire range. These discounts apply to case sales – six bottles or 12. Delivery is sometimes free if you tick the right box.

RED WINES

ARGENTINA

8 **Fragoso Merlot 2009** £6.49
Pleasant midweight plum-and-cherry party red.

8 **Vinalta Malbec 2009** £6.49
Straight unoaked, unblended Malbec of pleasing pliancy
with 14% alcohol.

AUSTRALIA

8 **One Chain The Opportunist Shiraz 2007** £6.74
Chocolate-and-chili centre to this dense, soupy, almost
spirity McLaren Vale monster (14.5% alcohol), and very
likeable. Online only.

7 **Snapper Cove Shiraz 2009** £6.99
Soupy, muscular barbecue red.

9 **Harrowgate Victoria Shiraz 2006** £8.99
Opulent-coloured dense oaked smoothie with 14.5%
alcohol is trimmed up with spice and acidity to make a
meaty but finely balanced whole.

8 **Knappstein Shady Grove**
Cabernet Sauvignon 2005 £16.00
Blood-coloured Clare Valley monster (14.5% alcohol) is
silky and even elegantly poised; an Aussie aristocrat worth
the money.

CHILE

8 **Soleado Merlot 2009** £4.29
Dark, dense new-squished blackberry fruit in this bouncing
bargain.

7 **Los Nucos Cabernet Sauvignon 2009** £4.99
Purple blackcurrancy young-tasting gripper with a
liquorice middle.

RED WINES

8 **Tierra Y Hombre Pinot Noir 2009** £6.49
Don't be put off by the pale colour, this is a generous (14.5% alcohol) raspberry-ripe Casablanca palate-refresher with a citrus tang; could serve cool.

8 **Corriente del Bio Pinot Noir 2009** £7.49
Very pale, strawberry-nosed, seductive soft fruit smoocher with a toffee background and 14% alcohol. Drink cool with chicken dishes.

8 **Los Molles Carmenère 2008** £7.99
It has the dense, rich, carmine colour that gives the grape its name, and corresponding dark, creamy fruit with a pinch of pepper; 14% alcohol.

CHILE

7 **Vin de Pays de l'Ardeche Gamay 2009** £3.99
I am cast down. This isn't a patch on the 2008, which I gave 10 points last year. Decent purple plonk, cheap.

8 **Gaston de Veau Rouge 2009** £4.99
Briary gripping Merlot-based Languedoc blend with layered flavours.

8 **Old Vines Grenache Noir 2008** £5.99
Soft, even sweet, easy-drinking Pyrenean party red with 14.5% alcohol.

9 **Les Orris Rouge 2007** £7.99
Plump, spicy and long Carignan/Grenache food red from Roussillon with mature oak richness and a keen edge.

FRANCE

9 **Piedmont Barbera 2009** £5.49
Fresh, brambly, bouncing affordable juicy pasta red made by Araldica. Love it.

ITALY

RED WINES

8 **Baglio Rosso Nero d'Avola**
Sicilia 2008 £5.99
Vigorous volcanic red with a crisp citrus rim; good food-matcher.

9 **Ripasso Valpolicella 2007** £7.99
Perennial souped-up Verona wine of irresistible ripeness, concentration and cherry essence. There's nothing quite like it with Italian meaty dishes.

8 **Merlot Friuli DOC Grave 2007** £9.99
'Chocolate and cherry,' it says in my note, to which 'sleek, juicy and even claret-like' needs adding.

9 **Umberto Fiore Barbaresco 2005** £9.99
Barbaresco at under a tenner is a rare thing, and this one is of real quality with orange rim, earthy, cherry perfume and toasty, nutty sweet fruit in a silky texture.

9 **Renato Ratti Nebbiolo Langhe 2007** £10.99
Endearing riverbank name has not helped this limpid, savoury poor-man's Barolo sell out since last year; I believe it's a better buy than most Barolo, and a bargain (14% alcohol).

8 **Kaituna Hills Reserve Pinot Noir 2008** £10.99
Dark raspberry-eucalyptus compote with silky oak and a nice green-pepper twang.

8 **Earth's End Pinot Noir 2008** £14.99
Unattractively packaged but delicious spare, pure, cherry-ripe style to this Central Otago luxury Pinot with 14% alcohol.

ITALY

NEW ZEALAND

RED WINES

S AFRICA

 7 **Charles Back Barbera 2008** £9.99
Nice brambly Cape spin on a familiar Italian (Asti) theme seems rather expensive; 14% alcohol.

SPAIN

 9 **Graciano Rioja 2006** £9.44
Not really Rioja, as it's 100% Graciano grapes but gloriously wild-fruit juicy plump brisk-finishing stuff by Bodegas Ondarre. Online only.

 8 **Rioja Pago Real 2007** £12.99
Dark purple reserva style with rich cassis fruit and 14% alcohol that will keep pace with the oak for years ahead. De luxe.

USA

 8 **Bonny Doon Mourvèdre 2008** £11.99
Savoury, gripping, opulently oaked fruits-of-the-forest Californian of character by cult winemaker Randal Grahm.

PINK WINES

ENGLAND

 7 **English Rosé 2009** £9.99
Onion-skin colour, bright with summer soft fruit and light in weight, but heavy on price.

FRANCE

7 **Gascogne Rosé 2009** £4.99
Confected colour, gobstopper smell, sweet lollipop flavour, and cheap. Bound to be popular.

ITALY

9 **La Prendina Estate Rosé 2009** £7.49
Best of all the M&S pinks, with discreet coral colour, floral whiff and beguiling strawberry fruit. Dry, but gutsy.

9 **Vinalta Chardonnay 2009**   £5.49
Nice gold colour, apple nose and straight mineral
unoaked fruit. Instantly charming and great value.

8 **Argentina Pinot Grigio 2009**   £6.49
Yellow, smoky, pungent, racily balanced friendly PG.

8 **Snapper Cove Chardonnay 2009**   £6.99
Old-fashioned Chardy has gold colour, rich but bright
aroma and dollops of peachy fruit.

8 **Margaret River Semillon Sauvignon 2008**   £7.99
Unoaked, bracing blend by Evans & Tate in the bordeaux
manner is strikingly fresh and stimulating.

8 **Fox Hollow Hunter Valley Verdelho 2008**   £9.99
Interesting aromatic vegetal-citrus refresher from a grape
once known only for Madeira. I warmed to it.

9 **Elqui PX 2009**   £4.99
A bracing orchard-fruit refresher from Pedro Ximinez, a
grape better known for the sweetest of sherries. Bargain.

10 **Tierra Y Hombre Sauvignon Blanc 2009**   £6.49
Chilean Sauvignon gets better and better, and here's a
scintillating example: crisp, tangy and grassy but also lush
and long. Tastes way above price.

8 **Secano Estate Sauvignon Gris 2009**   £7.49
Asparagus nose and matching fruit flavours in this
likeably exotic variation on the Sauvignon theme, with
14% alcohol.

**7 Sauvignon Blanc Vin de Pays
du Val de Loire 2009** £4.99
Bracing party white is good, clean fun – and cheap.

10 St Mont 2008 £6.49
This is a wonderful dry white from an obscure appellation
in the Gers, south-east of Bordeaux. It is lush and complex
and yet also slaking, mineral and brisk. Made by reliable
Plaimont co-operative.

8 Quincy Domaine Bailly 2008 £9.99
Satisfying stony-fresh Loire Sauvignon has a lick of
caramel in the background.

9 Pouilly Fumé Mathilde Favray 2008 £10.99
Lavish Loire Sauvignon has a fine enveloping seagrass-
fresh perfume and broad, intense fruit.

8 Grand Enclos de Château Cérons 2006 £14.99
Viscous de luxe Semillon-dominated dry bordeaux with
luxuriant tropical fruit and nifty limey edge. Pricy but
special.

**9 St Aubin 1er Cru Domaine
de Pimont Les Charmois 2006** £17.99
Grand Côtes de Beaune has extravagant nutty-creamy
aroma and apple-pie fruit. The real thing.

10 Palataia Pinot Grigio 2009 £6.99
The best PG on the market, this thrillingly aromatic, exotic
and smoky dry wine is at once delicate and assertive.
Benchmark successor to 2008, which scored 10 last year.

ITALY

8 Grave Sauvignon Friuli 2009 £6.99
Revealingly lively and tangy style to this unusual Venetian twist on the worldwide Sauvignon theme.

6 Prosecco Tranquillo 2009 £7.99
Whatever next? 'Tranquil' spin on eternal Prosecco theme is in fact a bit spritzy, and pear-like, with 11% alcohol.

8 Fiano Sannio 2008 £8.09
Rather green Campania wine is thrillingly stacked with layered orchard flavours. Only available online.

9 Pecorino Contesa 2009 £8.99
M&S introduced me to this lush Abruzzo white. Fine gold colour, exotic sub-tropical aromas and fruit, dry, crisp style. Name is of the grape variety; no cheese connection.

NEW ZEALAND

8 Shepherds Ridge Chardonnay 2008 £8.99
Ripe (14% alcohol) old-fashioned apple-pie-and-cream luxury Chardy by excellent Wither Hills winery in Marlborough.

**9 Kaituna Hills Reserve
Sauvignon Blanc 2009** £9.99
Shimmering flavours in this lovely nettly Montana (Marlborough) classic.

8 Te Muna Sauvignon Blanc 2008 £12.99
Crisp and green at the edge of the flavour and toffee note at the centre with lots of lush grassy fruit between.

S AFRICA

**8 Crow's Fountain Traditional Bush
Vine Sauvignon Blanc 2009** £8.99
Marked gooseberry style to this eager green food wine.

WHITE WINES

7 Knock On Wood Riesling Viognier 2009   £8.99
Rabbits adorn the label of this curiosity, which is redolent of banana and pineapple but actually does express the characteristics of both constituent grape varieties.

**9 Villiera Traditional Barrel-Fermented
Chenin Blanc 2009   £9.99**
Smells like a rich Coteaux du Layon but is quite dry, with a honeysuckle back taste to the vivacious fresh fruit; 14% alcohol.

8 Marmesa Chardonnay 2007   £9.86
Melons, peaches and no oak in this sunnily ripe, 14% alcohol pure-fruit Californian. Yummy, but available only online.

FORTIFIED WINES

8 Pink Port   £7.99
Violent magenta colour, but it does smell and even taste like proper port – sweet, not dry in the style of some white ports. Oddly likeable and 19% alcohol. Serve cold.

8 20-Year-Old Tawny Port   £29.99
Fiery, spicy, figgy and nutty – and seductively rich and silky too. Made by legendary David Guimaraens and quite expensive (20% alcohol).

8 M&S Fino Sherry   £5.99
Very pale and very pungent, even briny, fino but not fierce (15% alcohol).

FRANCE

9 De Saint Gall Champagne Brut Rosé   £24.99
Remarkably mellow onion-skin-coloured pink fizz is
hugely charming.

8 L'Avenue Rosé   £29.99
Alluring smoked-salmon colour and lots of summer fruit
in this long, intense, bright and lively mature champagne.

ITALY

8 Bellante Rosé   £8.99
Prosecco-style Treviso pink fizz has no Prosecco grapes in
it, but has a fresh strawberry appeal and 11% alcohol.

7 Le Contesse Prosecco   £8.99
Tastes like dry Asti Spumante, only with more alcohol,
at 11%.

Morrisons

 I have a problem with Morrisons. They hold wine tastings and don't invite me. The last one to which I was honoured to be asked was held in the autumn of 2009, and for all the time I was there – two to three hours – I was the only wine writer present. I was alone apart from the Morrisons team. I liked some of the wines, and enjoyed hearing about their origins and why the team had chosen them.

You'd have thought they would have been sufficiently pleased to see me to ask me to this year's tasting, but no. So, the entry in this edition has been contrived from wines I tasted all that time ago and wines I have bought from the shelves of Morrisons' branches.

My overall impression is that Morrisons takes less interest in its wine range than any of its rivals do. But I might be mistaken. I would just appreciate the chance to find out either way.

9 **Good French Cabernet Sauvignon 2008** £3.99

It is good, too, a densely coloured and concentrated vin de pays d'Oc with muscular blackcurrant fruit firmly in the Cabernet tradition, and good value.

8 **Good French Shiraz 2008** £3.99

Soupy-looking vin de pays d'Oc has nicely lifted spicy red fruit and long flavours; New World weight (and note Oz 'Shiraz' instead of French 'Syrah' on label), but French balance.

8 **Couleurs du Sud**
Cabernet Sauvignon 2008 £5.99

Grippy and satisfying vin de pays d'Oc is generous with its briar and spiciness.

8 **Crozes Hermitage Beaufeuil 2008** £8.99

Friendly pure-Syrah northern Rhône classic by Ogier – big new supplier to Morrisons – is already lipsmackingly ready to drink, and will develop.

9 **Château Cardinal Villemaurine 2002** £10.99

Super St Emilion Grand Cru in its prime has browning colour, heavenly cedary nose and silky classic-claret flavours incorporating plums, figs and black cherries, all finish with a textbook acidity.

9 **M The Best Montepulciano**
d'Abruzzo 2005 £5.60

I am a dedicated follower of this own-label regular, which is always several years older than any other supermarket counterpart. The 2005 is dark and thick with lashings of hedgerow fruit and an ideal nutskin-dry finish; great pasta wine.

FRANCE

ITALY

RED WINES

 Barolo Castiglione 2005 £9.99
Pale but not insubstantial; silky exotic fruit with a burnt-orange note and richness just short of raisiny; rare to find a decent Barolo under a tenner (if it still is); 14% alcohol.

 Barolo Cantine Gemma 2004 £13.69
More colour and density than usual in this ritzy number, in spite of its age; big sweetly ripe blackcurrant style with grippy finish, it's very grand and 14% alcohol.

 **Vergelegen Mill Race
Cabernet Sauvignon Merlot 2006** £9.69
Bordeaux-blend smoothie has well-defined varietal flavours and a silky richness that contrives to heighten, rather than hinder, the peaks in the flavour; 14.5% alcohol.

 **Namaqua Cabernet Sauvignon
Shiraz 2009 2l** £9.99
Please note, a 2-litre bag-in-box, at a tenner, equal to £3.75 a bottle, and it's a very pleasant, healthy, vigorous blend with 14% alcohol.

 M The Best Reserva Rioja 2004 £8.98
Pale, browning sweet-toffee-nosed old Rioja in genteel decline is comforting – the oak does not overwhelm the still-brambly fruit and there is a clean, brisk finish.

ITALY

SOUTH AFRICA

SPAIN

CHILE

9   **Mas O Menos Chardonnay 2009**   £3.99
Hugely ripe wine irresistibly evokes rhubarb and custard
to me, and all to the good. Lovely rich-but-dry Chardy at
a giveaway price with 14% alcohol.

7   **M The Best Chilean
          Sauvignon Blanc 2009**   £6.69
Very dry straight Sauvignon with briny-grassy freshness.

FRANCE

9   **Vouvray Première 2008**   £5.99
Banoffee pie comes to mind when sniffing this 'off-dry' Loire
Chenin Blanc, with its honey richness and lemon acidity
sandwiching lush peachy-banana fruit. Fine aperitif.

8   **Gewürztraminer Preiss Zimmer 2008**   £6.99
Gold-coloured powerful-lychee-scented Alsace exotic off-
dry white with gentle acidity.

8   **Vouvray Clos Palet 2008**   £6.99
Lemon-meringue pie this time! It calls itself 'demi-sec'
but is no sweeter than the Vouvray Première above. Nice
rich wine.

8   **Menetou-Salon Oscar Brillant 2008**   £8.99
Exciting tangy Loire Sauvignon with more than a hint of
tropical fruit amid the grassiness.

8   **Sancerre Fouassier 2008**   £9.98
Loire classic Sauvignon has a sherbet prickle and long
gooseberry-nettle style.

GERMANY

8   **M The Best Mosel Riesling**   £6.33
Non-vintage Spätlese-style has soft autumn ripeness but a
twang of racy acidity at the finish; 9% alcohol.

ITALY

8 M The Best Italian Pinot Grigio 2008 £5.97
Made by giant Cavit, a generously coloured, exotic, orchardy-smoky PG more in the Alsace style than expected. Actually, from Trentino.

NEW ZEALAND

8 Sacred Hill Sauvignon Blanc 2008 £9.29
Frisky, grassy classic Kiwi Sauvignon with contemplative depths. Above average in a field with very high standards. The 2009, tasted elsewhere, is its equal.

**8 Nobilo Limited Release
Sauvignon Blanc 2008** £9.99
Very green asparagus style from a brand better known for soft commercial stuff.

SPAIN

9 Moscatel de Valencia £3.48
Super stickie made from very late-harvested Muscat grapes with no spirit added (as in vin doux naturel) so just 10% alcohol and attractively pure grapey flavour. Good product.

ITALY

8 Prosecco Spumante Rosato £9.99
There's no predicting what you're going to like. This cynical concoction has a rose (flower, that is) aroma, bold strawberry fruit, friendly fizz and a clean dry style – and it genuinely pleases and refreshes.

Sainsbury's

Supermarkets like something new from time to time. Well, all of the time, really. New sells. In the way of these things, of course, it's as often as not just the packaging that's new. But as customers, most of us are easily taken in; we're just as eager to buy anything new as the supermarkets are to sell it to us.

So when the nice lady told me at the Sainsbury's tasting that they were launching 'a brand new own-label range of wines', I'll confess I was a tiny bit sceptical. But the proof is in the proverbial pudding. The range, of about 20 different reds, whites and rosés, has the simple umbrella name of 'House', as in the house wine of a restaurant. They are pitched at what in the trade is known as 'entry level', which means they are cheap – if any bottle of wine can be cheap when it's loaded with £2 of tax for starters.

'Our aim,' according to Sainsbury's, 'is for House to bring new customers into the wine category … by using grape varieties and wine styles that are easily recognisable, we hope to make shopping the wine aisle much easier, and an enjoyable experience.'

So I tried them, and they are quite extraordinarily good. The prices are incomprehensibly low. I even like the packaging. And yes, these wines are new. Two young Sainsbury's winemakers, Clem Yates and Barry Dick, have gone out into the world not just to source them, but to interfere in the way they are made, so they are just how they want them for the kind of customers who are new to the pleasures of wine.

In this Clem and Dick have succeeded. All the wines are non-vintage, meaning they are blends made from more than one harvest. This aids flexibility – to get a wine that tastes pleasingly fresh but not green, or mellow but still bright, mix together vats of different maturity and differing harvest conditions. It makes consistency easier, not being restricted to a single year, and no doubt it helps keep costs down.

Several of the wines are sold in three-litre bag-in-box format or as 1.5-litre PET (plastic) bottles at small pro rata savings on price. All the notes on the wines in the following pages are from tastings from standard bottles.

The House range apart, there continues to be an excellent choice of wine at Sainsbury's, with the perennial Taste the Difference range as inspiring as ever.

RED WINES

9 **Sainsbury's House Merlot** £3.49
Signature black-cherry style but with a nice gripping edge to the fruit, this is a healthy, balanced plump but clean food-matching red. The price is the mystery.

9 **Taste the Difference Barossa
Shiraz 2008** £7.99
Just about black in colour – like Marmite – and the concentration of flavour matches without being overdone. Big impact of porty richness (14% alcohol) but well-judged weight. Carnivores will love it.

8 **Willunga 100 Grenache 2007** £7.99
McLaren Vale barnstormer from the principal grape of the southern Rhône is sinuous, even chewy, and satisfying with 14.5% alcohol.

8 **Windy Peak Pinot Noir 2008** £7.99
Fresh lightly leafy classic pale Pinot by De Bortoli is good value.

10 **Gulf Station Pinot Noir 2008** £9.99
I gave this same wine 10 in last year's edition, and on retasting it is no less appealing: beautiful bricky colour, sweet enveloping cherry nose, super silky refined wine of mineral purity.

8 **Yering Station Shiraz Viognier 2007** £10.99
Dense, opaque, grippy, peppery black-fruit monster (14.5% alcohol) has nicely judged texture and weight.

8 **Sainsbury's House Red** £3.49
Legitimate Hérault party red is lively and clean.

AUSTRALIA

FRANCE

Sainsbury's (vertical side text)

FRANCE

10 Sainsbury's House Côtes du Rhône £3.69
Vivid green-edged spicy red fruit in the proper CdR mould. I can't fault it, or understand how they can bottle wine of this quality at such a price.

9 Sainsbury's House Claret £3.79
Quite dense youthful purply colour and matching density of blackcurrant and plum fruit; ripe and even smooth as if oaked (which it isn't). I am agog at the price.

9 Bouchard Aîné et Fils Pinot Noir 2008 £5.99
New World style Pinot of unexpectedly dense colour and bright but earthily convincing burgundy-method fruit. Seems cheap.

8 Chinon Domaine du Colombier 2008 £5.99
Typical leafy Loire Cabernet Franc with crunchy red fruit and super dry edge – great picnic red.

ITALY

9 Sainsbury's House Valpolicella £3.79
Light (11.5% alcohol) but by no means thin cherry-and-briar classic red has a fetching green-pepper aroma. The genuine article at an amazing price.

9 Sainsbury's House Chianti £3.86
Grippy raspberry-bramble midweight chianti of recognisable style has pale colour but well-set ripe fruit; good pasta/pizza red at an unheard-of price.

8 Taste the Difference Primitivo 2008 £6.49
From Salice Salentino, a rather sophistictaed Primitivo with coffee and spice notes in the black fruit and a bitter-chocolate centre.

8 Piccini Chianti Superiore 2008 £7.99
Dense and rich cherry fruit introduced by a citrus note with underlying liqueur chocolate. Good, firm, complicated stuff.

RED WINES

8 **San Colombaio Vino**
Nobile di Montepulciano 2007   £10.99
Blood red with correspondingly intense plummy-minty
fruit – classic vino nobile at a decent price.

8 Taste the Difference Amarone 2007   £15.03
Unfeasibly dark and dense valpolicella variation made
with dried grapes is marvellously juicy and concentrated,
almost raisiny, and 14.5% alcohol; an acquired taste
worth acquiring.

9 Taste the Difference Barolo 2005   £15.49
As usual, a pale colour going orange at the rim, a spirity-
nutty aroma and poised cherry-plum fruit with a nutskin-
dry edge; but in the round, an unusually elegant and
satisfying mature Barolo, for once worth the money.

8 **Sacred Hill Hawke's Bay**
Syrah 2008   £8.99
Cool, intense, slinky-spicy black-fruit red with discreet
oak.

8 Taste the Difference Douro 2008   £7.52
The colour and nose bring port to mind and the sleek,
savoury, rich-cassis fruit doesn't let you down.

8 Taste the Difference
South African Shiraz 2008   £7.99
You do taste the difference, because this is immediately
identifiable as a Cape wine, a dark, tarry, peppery but
friendly fruit bomb with 14.5% alcohol.

ITALY

N ZEALAND

PORTUGAL

S AFRICA

Red Wines

Spain

🍷 **8** **Sainsbury's House Cabernet Sauvignon** £3.49
With the world to choose from, Spain seems an unlikely source for a sub £3.50 Cabernet, but it's a good, vigorous, blackcurrant wine finishing nicely.

Pink Wines

🍷 **8** **Sainsbury's Rosé d'Anjou 2009** £3.99
Shameless shocking pink sweet softie with strawberry fruit – a ripe and healthy bargain with 11% alcohol.

🍷 **8** **Sainsbury's Prestige Cuvée**
Côtes du Rhône Rosé 2009 £4.68
Sounds grand, but a nifty bargain, this is a bright magenta Grenache pink with dry, focused and refreshing strawberry flavours.

🍷 **8** **Taste the Difference**
Côtes de Provence Rosé 2009 £7.99
Pale salmon pink, dry but softly ripe strawberry style to this Grenache-based refresher.

White Wines

France

🍷 **8** **Taste the Difference**
Adelaide Hills Chardonnay 2008 £7.99
Straight apple-peachy style with a nice bit of toasty oak, it's appealingly pure and comforting, with 14% alcohol.

🍷 **7** **Yalumba Y Series Viognier 2009** £7.99
Good citrus lift at the finish of this dry, apricot-scented wine.

🍷 **8** **D'Arenberg The Olive Grove**
Chardonnay 2007 £8.99
From a McLaren Vale winery known for serious wines with silly names, a big, dimensional Chardy with a mélange of ripe fruit flavours and 14% alcohol.

Australia

CHILE

7 Castillo de Molina Sauvignon Blanc 2009   £7.99
Seagrass aroma jumps from the glass, though the fruit is
unexpectedly understated, with a softness that will appeal
to those who don't like their Sauvignon too green.

**8 Sainsbury's Premières
Côtes de Bordeaux 37.5cl   £3.49**
Flowery, honeyed and balanced pudding wine of genuine
quality.

8 Sainsbury's Anjou Blanc 2009   £4.79
'Off-dry' asserts the label, but it's merely dry to my way of
thinking, though with a twist of honey in the background.
Fresh, brisk Chenin Blanc with just 10.5% alcohol.

8 Jacques Lurton Sauvignon Blanc 2009   £4.99
Brisk but not eye-watering Loire gooseberry bargain with
just 11.5% alcohol.

FRANCE

**8 Blason de Bourgogne
Mâcon-Villages 2009   £5.99**
Fine lemon-gold colour and authentic stony melon-peach
Mâconnais Chardonnay style.

**9 Taste the Difference
Mâcon-Villages 2009   £5.99**
This is made by the same Blason co-op as the branded
Mâcon above; tasting them together, I found this one
richer in colour and riper in fruit – but are the two wines
the same?

**8 Taste the Difference
Muscadet Sèvre et Maine Sur Lie 2009   £6.29**
Lick of honey on the nose of this bone-dry but generously
fruity Loire moules-matcher. Acidity just right – none of
the green tartness that can mar these wines.

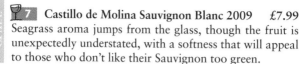

8 Taste the Difference
Alsace Gewürztraminer 2008   £7.29
Standard Turckheim co-op stuff but with intriguing
lychee nose, sweet exotic fruit and a nice grapefruit
twang, it's delightful if not different.

8 Taste the Difference Petit Chablis 2009   £7.49
Zingy but intense frisky-flinty Chardonnay from a
disappearing AC tastes very much like grown-up Chablis.

8 Alsace Riesling Vieilles Vignes 2007   £8.99
Exotic stony but lush Cave de Turckheim product has rich
colour, satisfying weight and nicely controlled ripeness.

10 Taste the Difference Pouilly Fumé 2009   £9.99
This is becoming an institution: lovely new vintage with
long, lush herbaceous Sauvignon flavours in the best Loire
tradition. Compares to the best of the Kiwi pretenders.

8 Sancerre La Porte de Caillou 2009   £10.99
Nice pebbly-grassy Loire classic Sauvignon that I preferred
to the pricier Taste the Difference Sancerre.

9 Chablis Premier Cru Sélection
Domaines Brocard 2008   £12.99
Well-coloured Côte d'Or-style Chablis with lavish but
unoaked Chardonnay fruit with lovely mineral purity.

9 Sainsbury's House Soave   £3.29
Crisp balance of almonds and apples in this excellent dry
Verona wine at an implausible price.

8 Sainsbury's Sicilian White   £3.66
Aromatic orchard-fruit off-dry island white of real charm
is a bargain.

8 Sainsbury's House Pinot Grigio   £4.29
Well-made Trentino PG of impressive flavour and freshness.

8 **Sanctuary Sauvignon Blanc 2009** £6.99
Green, nettly style with gentle acidity is easy to enjoy.

9 **Sacred Hill Marlborough**
Sauvignon Blanc 2009 £8.99
If anything, even better than the lush 2008, this is bright
and intense with grassy-lemony highlights. From a Wairau
Valley vineyard called Hell's Gate, it stands out.

9 **Taste the Difference Albariño 2009** £6.99
Dependable tangy dry wine from Rias Baixas has some
of the style of Sauvignon but remains utterly distinctive
and a grand match for seafood and creamy-sauce dishes
of all kinds.

9 **Sainsbury's Blanc de Noirs Champagne** £17.29
After years of being lauded here, this remarkably consistent
champagne has been winning all kinds of awards, and
rightly so. The label has been redesigned but the wine is
still in the same generous, toasty, ripe and mature-tasting
style as ever.

8 **First Cape Limited Release**
Sparkling Rosé £5.99
Lurid colour, lively fizz, bold strawberry fruit – better than
I expected!

Tesco

The 2010 tasting season got off to a bad start for me. The Tesco event was the first in the calendar, and I missed it by turning up to the wrong venue and failing to make contact with anyone at Tesco HQ who might know the correct address. They were all, of course, at the tasting.

My wife was kind, in the circumstances, when I got home. 'You'll just have to buy all the wines you would have tasted,' she said. Not all at once, but progressively through the months in the run-up to Best Wines in the Supermarkets 2011's production schedule. And that's what I've done. The good ones have been a treat, and the less-good ones a sorrow, having been obtained at some expense. It's been salutary. When you've paid for wine that disappoints, it hurts. And it's a reminder to me of the responsibility I bear in producing this book.

At the last minute, Tesco saved the day to some degree by announcing a tenth-anniversary tasting of its Finest range of wines. There was just time to attend the event (I went to the right place this time), and it was well worth the journey.

Finally, a word about www.tesco.com. Most of the wines in the stores are available by the case (six bottles as often as 12) and there are many online exclusives. Mixed-case offers are perpetual and numerous, and discounts legion. It is fantastically efficient. Place your order before noon on any weekday, and they deliver the next morning.

RED WINES

ARGENTINA

8 **Finest Argentinian Mendoza Malbec 2008** £6.99
Near-black colour and brûlée fruit with pruny highlights make for a reassuring winter red with 14% alcohol.

AUSTRALIA

8 **Finest Howcroft Estate Cabernet Sauvignon 2009** £7.99
Pure blackcurranty Limestone Coast wine is nicely defined and clean, and 14% alcohol.

9 **Finest Yarra Valley Pinot Noir 2007** £13.99
Silky, supple, balanced Pinot of extraordinary charm. I had not a moment's doubt it's worth the money.

CHILE

7 **Yali Cabernet Sauvignon Carmenère 2008** £6.49
Environmentally correct light blend has pleasant redcurrant fruit.

7 **Finest Organic Colchagua Valley Pinot Noir 2009** £7.49
Slinky cherry-peppery chicken-matcher with good ripeness (14% alcohol) and grip, if a tad pricy.

FRANCE

8 **Finest Beaujolais-Villages 2009** £5.98
Perky and recognisable glugger to serve cool.

8 **Tesco Côtes du Rhône Villages Reserve 2008** £5.99
Handsomely presented dark and spicy winter red from prolific Gabriel Meffre; 14% alcohol.

FRANCE

10   **Finest Red Burgundy 2008**   **£6.99**
If you want to get to know burgundy, start here. This beautifully expressive Pinot Noir from the villages of Chambolle Musigny, Santenay and Chassagne Montrachet is typically light in colour and weight, but wonderfully firm and defined with its cherry, raspberry and strawberry fruit with a proper burgundian earthiness. A gift at the price.

8   **Finest Vin de Pays d'Oc Malbec 2009**   **£6.99**
Bruiser has leathery edge to aroma, lipsmacking black fruit, and could do with a year or two to mellow.

8   **Finest Vin de Pays Côtes Catalans Grenache 2009**   **£6.99**
Inky, brambly, grippy monster is attractively packaged and agreeably savoury.

9   **Finest Gérard Bertrand Tautavel 2005**   **£7.99**
Muscular Roussillon has liquorice intensity to its mellow but still-tannic black fruit. Special wine from a hugely ripe and mature vintage at a good price.

10   **Finest St Emilion 2008**   **£7.99**
Claret as it ought to be: dark and inviting in colour and aroma, with an expensive blackberry-cedary-minty character; mostly Merlot, it is silky and thoroughly well-developed in spite of its youthfulness, and a textbook wine of its kind at a price I find hard to compute.

8   **Finest Crozes Hermitage 2007**   **£8.49**
Plenty of weight, for once, in this cherry-with-stone-in northern Rhône red.

8   **Laurent Miquel Heritage Vineyards Syrah 2008**   **£8.49**
Healthy bright and spicy Languedoc with rather lavish oak notes.

10 Finest Gigondas 2007 £12.49
This wine is simply gorgeous, hugely dark, concentrated, silky, spicy and opulent, perfectly balanced in spite of 15% alcohol, and ready to drink now – or any time over the next decade. I also tasted the 2008, which was lean and weedy by comparison. Seek out the 2007 while it lasts.

8 Finest Nuits St Georges 2007 £18.99
Peppered-raspberry nose, pale colour and a crunchy fruit somehow coalesce into a scrumptious burgundy that will develop over years to come; expensive, though.

9 Finest Hermitage 2005 £19.99
The point is that this is the real thing. It might just be from the local co-op, the Cave de Tain, but it's proper Hermitage with dense, brooding (and browning) colour, authentic gamey pong and epic Syrah creamy-but-not-sweet fruit.

FRANCE

9 Finest Valpolicella Ripasso 2008 £6.49
Big, soft but grippy black-cherry Valpolicella variation with plumskin dryness to match meaty dishes. Good value.

9 Finest Nero d'Avola Sicilia 2008 £6.49
Grippingly ripe, dark food red with convincing Sicilian-spice and bitter chocolate centre from a grape native to the island.

10 Finest Barbera d'Asti 2007 £6.99
Consistently brilliant Piedmont blueberry-fruit juicy quencher made by giant producer Fratelli Martini is equally consistently on promo at about a fiver – and it is on this admittedly uncertain principle that I have given it a maximum score.

ITALY

RED WINES

8 Chianti Riserva 2007   **£7.29**
Identifiable Chianti with silky fruit and nutty dryness is
nicely defined and balanced.

8 Monte Nobile Squinzano Riserva 2006   **£8.99**
Gaudy heraldic label and endearing Puglian DOC name
make this an attractive bottle before the screwcap is even
off; inside, it's a sunny-ripe, chocolate-smooth blackberry
slurper of huge charm.

**8 Famiglia Torraccia Chianti
Riserva 2006**   **£10.99**
Insinuating cherry-raspberry mature Chianti with a caramel
touch and nifty nutskin finish is far too expensive at £10.99
but one to seek out at regular half-price discount.

9 Finest Barolo 2005   **£15.49**
Handsomely labelled Ascheri Giacomo classic has big tar-
and-roses nose, rich colour going orange, and substantial,
elegant fruit. Price is forgivable.

8 Ricossa Barolo 2004   **£20.00**
Online only at wildly fluctuating discounts, this is an
unusually dense example with cherries, roses, coffee and
grip; a bargain at the £8 I paid as part of a mixed case.

8 Finest Marlborough Pinot Noir 2009   **£9.49**
Pale, eager, cherry-strawberry lightweight is a serious
wine, bright and stimulating; I'd serve it cool.

8 Finest Touriga Nacional 2008   **£6.99**
Endearing jampot label on this Lisbon wine, which has a
hint of port about it, with clove and plum amid the dark,
savoury fruit.

ITALY

N ZEALAND

PORTUGAL

RED WINES

SOUTH AFRICA

10 **Finest Beyers Truter Pinotage 2008** £7.99
This is the Pinotage I've been waiting for. It's pitch dark and very dense but beautifully poised with spicy, plummy fruit, and perfectly weighted. It wears its 14.5% alcohol lightly, and the price seems about half what it's worth.

9 **Finest Stellenbosch Shiraz 2008** £7.99
Spicy and dark, long and lush, a superbly weighted Sunday roast red with 14% alcohol and 100% charm.

9 **Gran Tesoro Garnacha 2008** £3.62
Still on shelf, the 08 of this cheapie has mellowed from last year's note of 'lively, spicy young' to inky, spicy, juicy and rounded. A snip.

9 **Limited Edition Finest Valdepeñas Gran Reserva 2000** £6.99
Lovely lacy old La Mancha anniversary wine has the fruit well on top of the vanilla oak, and a modest price.

SPAIN

9 **Finest Old Vines Tempranillo 2009** £6.99
Full, generous blackberry juice bomb is well defined and finishes crisply. Such a good food red – anything meaty – and 14% alcohol.

9 **Finest Viña Mara Rioja Reserva 2005** £7.00
Dense burnt-orange colour and a big, sweet nose with vanilla, coffee and rose petals lead into a lovely toothsome de luxe Rioja at an alluring price.

10 **Limited Edition Finest Viña Mara Rioja Gran Reserva 2000** £9.99
Colour of this great anniversary Rioja by Baron de Ley is still ruby, and the fruit is correspondingly blushing, ripe and vivid with the rich oak firmly in the supporting role. A miraculous Rioja of timeless character and balance, at a giveaway price.

RED WINES

SPAIN

9 **Limited Edition Finest Ribera del Duero Gran Reserva 2000** £14.99

Sherry whiff off this gorgeous, insinuating, minty-eucalypt dense pure Tempranillo with the benefit of bottle age. A rare chance to try the classic style at a defendable price.

PINK WINES

FRANCE

8 **Finest Gérard Bertrand Grenache Rosé 2009** £5.99

Pale but generously fruity dry, soft and easy Languedoc pink.

7 **Finest Côtes de Provence Rosé 2009** £8.99

Pale salmon colour, defined freshness with a hint of toffee. Pricey.

SPAIN

8 **Finest Navarra Rosé 2009** £6.49

Shocking pink, and a good impact of strawberry fruit, too, in this robust refresher.

WHITE WINES

8 **Finest Dessert Semillon 2005** £6.29

Nicely judged, gold-coloured, elegantly weighted, honeyed sweetie with trim acidity and 10% alcohol.

AUSTRALIA

8 **Finest Denman Vineyard Semillon 2006** £7.99

Mature wine has gold colour, canned-fruit-salad nose and insinuating lusciousness, but it is dry and lively, and has just 10.5% alcohol.

8 **Finest Tingleup Riesling 2009** £7.99

Broad-flavoured dry style to this grapefruit cocktail with less lime than some Aussie Rieslings, but plenty of refreshment.

9 Finest High Eden Chardonnay 2008 £12.99
Rich in every dimension, an extravagant de luxe wine from grand Mountadam (Barossa) vineyards, this ideally combines fullness and freshness, with 14% alcohol.

9 Limited Edition Finest Hunter
Valley Semillon 2000 £15.99
Yellow, petrolly, pineapple-sweet food wine is dry, really, and just 10% alcohol, but a fascinating insight into how well-made Aussie Semillon can evolve. Special.

8 Finest Tapiwey Sauvignon Blanc 2010 £8.99
Breezily expressive Casablanca wine with long, grassy-fresh flavours.

8 Tesco White Burgundy 2008 £5.48
Light, apple-fresh Chardonnay with a fleeting caramel richness. Cheap for burgundy.

8 Finest Alsace Pinot Gris 2008 £6.99
Well-coloured exotic tropical-spicy dry wine has weight and ripeness.

8 Finest Vin de Pays de Gascogne Gros
Manseng Sauvignon Blanc 2009 £6.99
Gascony's not famed for fascinating wines, but this one is a peach: plush, fresh, autumn flavours and just 11.5% alcohol.

8 Finest Vin de Pays d'Oc Grenache
Marsanne 2009 £6.99
Big, ripe sunny blend is plump with rich orchard fruit, and has decided impact.

8 Finest White Burgundy 2009   £6.99
Good colour and an almondy richness in this creamy-oaked
Chardonnay from famed Buxy winery at Montagny.

8 Finest Alsace Gewürztraminer 2008   £7.29
Gold colour, strong lychee-ginger nose on this intense but
not overdone spice bomb.

9 Finest Chablis 2009   £8.94
Immediately attractive and identifiable Chablis of steely
but easy charm. Stands out.

9 Finest Sauternes 2005 37.5cl   £12.29
Deep gold classic Sauternes with honeyed botrytis
character and nifty balance is fair value.

8 Finest Chablis Premier Cru 2008   £13.29
Loved this fine, flinty-but-rich wine, which will mellow
with time.

8 Finest Steillage Riesling 2008   £6.29
Light lemony Moselle at 11.5% alcohol has a stony
freshness and proper Riesling raciness. Reasonable price.

8 Finest Trentino Pinot Grigio 2009   £5.99
Nice smoky, flavourful dry example by giant Cavit.

8 Finest Fiano 2009   £5.99
Ideal balance of brassica and ripeness in this Sicilian
perennial.

8 Finest Gavi 2009   £6.99
Lots of fruit and blanched almond in this extra-ripe
new vintage.

FRANCE

GERMANY

ITALY

ITALY

9   **Finest Vermentino 2009**   £6.99
Brand new Sicilian has a marginally confected nose but delicate, fleeting ripe fruit and a slurp of richness at the centre. Grows on you.

NEW ZEALAND

8   **Finest Marlborough
Sauvignon Blanc 2009**   £6.49
Stacks of grass and gooseberry in this long, easy-drinking refresher at a modest price.

8   **Finest Marlborough Autumn
Pick Riesling 2009**   £8.99
The sweetness comes right through to give a truly authentic autumn ripeness to this racy aperitif, with just 9.5% alcohol.

S. AFRICA

7   **Finest Darling Sauvignon Blanc 2009**   £7.49
Prominent 'Darling' on label will attract some shoppers to this big, soft, long-flavoured, mild-acidity Sauvignon.

8   **Finest Ken Forrester Chenin Blanc 2009**   £9.49
Dry but exotic part-oaked aperitif dry wine mixes fresh fruit with sweet nuttiness.

SPAIN

10   **Finest Albariño 2009**   £6.99
From prodigious Rias Baixas region, you get a lot of gold colour and intense grassy, green-but-lush seaside freshness for the money. I think these Spanish wines are the most refreshing on the planet.

9   **Finest Rueda Verdejo 2009**   £6.99
Bright, breezy, brassica-crisp refresher delivers flavours and sensations that linger in the mind.

AUSTRALIA

**8 Limited Edition Finest 10 Year Old
Grand Tawny 2000**   **£8.99**
Cheeky Aussie tilt at tawny port from Grenache, Shiraz
and Mataro grapes is Madeira-coloured, very sweet,
fruitcake rich and fun, with 19% alcohol.

PORTUGAL

9 Finest 10 Year Old Tawny Port   **£11.99**
Rich copper colour, intense spirity-figgy nose and a luscious
balance of fire and fruit in this well-married Symington
port at 20% alcohol.

8 Finest Vintage Port 1994   **£16.49**
Would you lay down Tesco port? Either way, this
Symington vintage is coming round nicely, with deep ruby
colour, coffee and fruitcake aromas and big sweet flavours
with 20% alcohol. Will last a decade or more yet.

8 Finest Vintage Champagne 2004   **£18.99**
At the same price as the less-inspiring non-vintage 'Premier
Cru', a generous, bready, all-Chardonnay fizz with an
uplifting lemon-zest style.

FRANCE

**9 Limited Edition Finest Champagne
Chanoine 2000**   **£24.99**
Soft, creamy but crisply finishing mature anniversary
champagne of real appeal.

ITALY

8 Bisol Prosecco di Valdobbiadene   **£9.99**
Dry and busily fizzy with a likeable sherbet-fresh, peary
fruit, this is bright and refreshing.

Waitrose

France has sunk to fifth place, behind Australia, the US, Italy and South Africa as a supplier of wine to UK retailers, but at Waitrose the French are still number one. This might merely reveal Waitrose's wine buyers as a pack of old reactionaries, but I like to think of it as firm evidence that Waitrose knows its customers, and gives them what they want. There is certainly no other supermarket with a French wine range that remotely equals that of Waitrose. Where else would you find both the best red vin de pays bargain on the market, Cuvée de Chasseur 2009 at £3.99 (it scores 10 in this edition) and one of the grandest grand cru classé clarets of them all, Château Léoville Las Cases 2003 at a mere £166.25? The latter wine makes no appearance in this edition as I have not been privileged to taste it, but I think you'll get the drift.

Waitrose does enjoy a uniquely upmarket profile, but I am entirely convinced that its wine range competes on even terms with all its rivals. I have picked out a dozen sub-£5 wines this year for terrific quality and value among the 100 featured on the following pages – by a mile the longest entry in this edition and, yes, a genuine representation of just how various and good value the Waitrose offering is.

Most of the wines mentioned here should be found in the stores – now 228 of them throughout the country – but some I have noted as Waitrose Direct buys, which means available only online or by phone on 0800 188881. The website is a good one, and you can buy the full range ('more than 1,200 wines, spirits and champagnes'), mixing your own cases.

Other supermarket sites (barring Booths) insist you buy by the unmixed or pre-mixed case.

You do need to buy a minimum of 12 bottles, though, any mix, to qualify for free delivery. And here's a promise from Alex Murray, manager of Waitrose Wine Direct: 'You can now order up to 7pm and still get your wines delivered before 10.30am the next day.' Go on, take him at his word.

RED WINES

ARGENTINA

**9 Familia Zuccardi FuZion
Shiraz/Malbec 2009** £5.19
It really is a fusion of fruit and firmness – a generous,
grippy young red at a keen price.

**8 Fairtrade Tilimuqui Cabernet
Sauvignon/Bonarda 2009** £6.65
Strong (but modest 13% alcohol), dark and spicy well-
made and well-intentioned Famatina Valley food red.

7 Brown Brothers Tarrango 2008 £6.49
Pale, Ribena-style, quirky, dry-finishing, lightweight
picnic red to drink cool.

AUSTRALIA

**8 Finca Flichman Reserve
Oak-Aged Malbec 2009** £7.19
Stonking (14% alcohol) sweet pruny red is long and juicy

9 Waitrose Reserve Shiraz 2008 £8.99
From the redoubtable St Hallett winery in the Barossa, a
pitch-dark, rich but balanced blackberry-cassis red of real
character with 14.5% alcohol.

**8 Wirra Wirra Church Block Cabernet
Sauvignon/Shiraz/Merlot 2008** £10.99
Pepper-the-target blend has reassuring leather whiff,
dark well-upholstered deep spicy blackfruit flavours and
14.5% alcohol. Dependable old friend.

CHILE

8 Virtue Merlot/Cabernet Sauvignon 2009 £4.19
Eco-wine of soft, agreeable briary style is jolly good value.

**8 Los Unidos Fairtrade Carmenère/Cabernet
Franc 2009** £6.19
Nicely edged firm blackcurranty blend has fresh-fruit appeal.

RED WINES

CHILE

8 **Concha y Toro Sunrise Merlot 2009** £6.29
Plump and ripe 'entry-level' red from Chile's dominant
producer has healthy, lipsmacking juiciness.

8 **Mont Gras Reserva Carmenère 2009** £8.19
Familiar brand excels with this brightly purple briary
chocolate-hearted vanilla-oaked nicely integrated
smoothie with 14.5% alcohol.

10 **Cono Sur Reserva Merlot 2008** £8.99
Simply fabulous minty, dense, plush, perfectly weighted
14% alcohol big brand that in this vintage hits the spot.
It aspires successfully to the elegance of Bordeaux, with a
luscious ripeness all its own.

9 **Tabali Encantado Reserva Syrah 2008** £10.99
Lovely slinky-spicy oaked style has huge black fruit
(14.5% alcohol) with sultry savour and edgy tannins.
Good now, but must have years of evolution ahead.

FRANCE

10 **Cuvée de Chasseur 2009** £3.99
'It is arguably my cheapest wine that I am most amazed by,
the loyal Cuvée de Chasseur, a veritable beacon of value.' So
says Waitrose buyer Andrew Shaw of this plump, healthy,
blackberry perennial southern vin de pays. I agree entirely.

8 **Classic Côtes du Rhône 2009** £4.49
Bright and vivid red-fruit cheapie with a pinch of white
pepper is good value.

8 **Corbières Réserve de la Perrière 2008** £4.69
Gripping, spicy Mediterranean food wine from an
appellation that can be coarse. This one stands out for
intensity and suppleness.

Red Wines

9 Saumur Les Nivières 2009   **£6.99**
Elegantly weighted Loire wine is deliciously expressive
of the lush, leafy Cabernet Franc grape, a red wine that
refreshes in every sense.

**8 Minervois Gérard Bertrand
Syrah/Grenache 2007**   **£6.99**
Winter-fuel purple red is meaty and robust with suggestions
of cinnamon, thyme and pepper; 14% alcohol.

**8 Calvet Reserve Merlot-Cabernet
Sauvignon 2008**   **£7.99**
Big wine under a big Bordeaux brand name is deep purple
with substantial, rounded blackcurrant fruit. Regularly
discounted, a true bargain to look out for.

9 Faugères Domaine Marie 2009   **£7.99**
Perfectly lush deep-purple juicy spicy-minty Mediterranean
red with wafts of the garrigue and a sublime weight.

8 Georges Duboeuf Chiroubles 2009   **£8.99**
Firm, structured Beaujolais cru suggests 2009 is a lovely
ripe vintage with wines that will evolve, including this one.

**8 Domaine de la Croix de Chaintres
Saumur Champigny 2008**   **£9.99**
Grippy-leafy typical Loire red with good weight of
purple, dark berry fruit. Nice definition makes it a great
match to starchy or fatty foods.

**8 Château Cesseras Minervois
La Livinière 2007**   **£12.99**
Blood red Mediterranean monster has lavish red fruit,
spicy depths and mature roundness; 14% alcohol.
Waitrose Direct.

RED WINES

**Gigondas Patrick Lesec
Les Espalines 2007**   £14.99
Huge (15.5% alcohol) Rhône with a complex melange of black fruit.

**Monthélie 1er Cru Les Riottes
Vincent Girardan 2007**   £19.99
Pure-silk burgundy from a tiny Volnay neighbour is worth the price. Waitrose Direct.

Château Larrivet Haut-Brion 2004   £24.99
Extraordinary Graves (Bordeaux) prestige wine from an overlooked vintage is oloroso colour with a rich, cigar-box nose and ripe, mature classic-claret fruit with figgy oak.

FRANCE

**Tsantali Organic Cabernet
Sauvignon 2006**   £8.49
A rabbit out of the hat. From Halkidiki in Greece's Balkan north, a wildly delicious, ripe-cassis, mature, silky Cabernet with 14.5% alcohol but beautifully balanced between power and purity. Drink this wine and save Greece!

GREECE

Saluti Rosso 2009   £4.99
Brisk redcurrant pasta wine from Nero d'Avola, Sangiovese and Syrah grapes sourced in Sicily.

Vignale Valpolicella 2009   £4.99
Fully fruity cherry-bright rendering of the old Verona favourite is plump and ripe – a very pleasant surprise at the price.

**Barbera d'Asti Superiore
Vincio-Vaglio I Tre Vescovi 2007**   £7.99
Juicy and unexpectedly weighty plummy bouncer with rather extravagant richness. You'll warm to it.

ITALY

RED WINES

ITALY

9 **Waitrose Ripasso di Valpolicella Classico Superiore Fratelli Recchia 2006** £9.99
Quirky Valpolicella variation has dark-hearted mellow cherry fruit and weighty intensity with 14.5% alcohol. Try with cured meats and pongy cheese.

N ZEALAND

8 **Craggy Range Merlot 2007** £12.99
Lush, integrated blackberry smoothie is immediately impressive, with 14.5% alcohol – Kiwi Pétrus?

PORTUGAL

8 **Dão Pena de Pato 2007** £6.99
Firm, pruny red with crisp edge to match oily fish, especially sardines.

8 **Tinta da Anfora 2007** £7.29
Perennial Alentejo in yet another excellent vintage is dark and savoury, highly individual in that eucalypt, spicy Portuguese way, and 14% alcohol.

8 **Arco do Esporão 2008** £9.99
I thought I detected a pomegranate note amid the spice of this delicious, concentrated dark-fruit Alentejo red with 14% alcohol.

8 **Cortes de Cima Syrah 2005** £10.99
Pure Syrah but distinctly Portuguese with its exotic minty-herbaceous notes amidst lush, rich, oaked dark flavours; 14% alcohol.

S AFRICA

9 **Zalze Shiraz/Mourvèdre/Viognier 2009** £6.49
Brambly monster (14.5% alcohol) of near-black colour has a pleasingly comfortable weight and a bright freshness of fruit. Charming, and cheap.

RED WINES

SOUTH AFRICA

9 **Southern Right Pinotage 2008** £11.99
Named after the Southern Right whales that are seen in Walker Bay, location (one mile inland) of the vineyard, this is an exceptional minty-roasted-liquorous oaked Pinotage befitting the price.

8 **Boekenhoutskloof The Chocolate Block 2008** £16.99
Jumbo spicy, Syrah-based dance-on-your-tongue, silky-oaked 15% alcohol red-meat-matcher doesn't evoke chocolate, but has a proper fruit-and-nut centre.

SPAIN

7 **Gran López Tinto Campo de Borja 2009** £4.79
Perky Garnacha-Tempranillo party blend with a decidely firm finish and 14% alcohol.

8 **Viña Herminia Rioja Crianza 2005** £8.29
Convincing vanilla-raspberry balance in this rather plush mature Rioja with 14% alcohol.

8 **Chivite Gran Feudo Navarra Tempranillo/ Cabernet Sauvignon/Merlot 2005** £11.99
Whopping stalwart dark plummy fruit bomb from underrated Navarra, neighbour to Rioja.

9 **Viña Arana Rioja Alta Reserva 2001** £19.99
Antique has a lovely ruby-orange colour, high-toned near-spirity aroma ('haunting', I foolishly noted) and delicate but well-defined classic Rioja fruit. Fabulous, which it needs to be at the price.

USA

7 **Virtue Californian Red 2009** £4.19
New eco-wine (bulk-shipped, lightened glass UK bottle, etc) is light, quite sweet, but healthy-tasting.

10 Brown Brothers Moscato Rosa 2009 £6.49
Smoked-salmon colour and tingly bit of spritz in this
delightful grapey contrivance with just 7% alcohol but
masses of interest. It is not quite a sweet wine, but a
charming one. I've tasted nothing else quite like it.

**9 Miguel Torres San Medin
Cabenet Sauvignon Rosé 2009** £7.29
Bubblegum colour to this consistent zingy-crunchy summer
soft-fruit cooler. Fine minerality.

8 Champteloup Rosé d'Anjou 2009 £6.15
Loire pink has smoked salmon colour, floral nose and
a strawberry ripeness just short of sweet with just 11%
alcohol.

8 Esprit de Buganay Rosé 2009 £8.49
Pale pink Côtes de Provence has elegant floral perfume
and dry but intense summer soft fruit.

8 Italia Pinot Grigio Rosé 2009 £6.49
Liked this in spite of misgivings about pink wines made
from white-wine grapes. The colour comes from added
Pinot Noir, is a perky magenta and there is keen, fresh
raspberry fruit.

8 Vida Nova Rosé 2009 £8.49
Lurid fresh generous strawberry-grapefruit dry refresher
from Sir Cliff Richard's Algarve estate.

**9 Zalze Cabernet Sauvignon/Shiraz
Rosé 2009** £6.49
Strong attractive colour, emphatic ripe berry fruit, 14%
alcohol, dry and refreshing, and a good price.

**8 Marquesa de la Cruz Garnacha
Rosé 2009** £7.15
Big colour, 14% alcohol, reducurrant Campo de Borja
food-matching rosé with crunchy freshness.

9 **Googee Bay Semillon/Chardonnay 2009** £4.99
Yellow, plump, autumn-fruit bargain of great charm.
Ignore the naff label.

8 **De Bortoli DB Selection Verdelho 2009** £6.29
Likeable fruit-salad Riverina dry has a keen raciness as well
as lush oaky notes – just the thing with Asian recipes.

7 **Yalumba Organic Viognier 2009** £7.99
Amid the ocean of flabby sweet Viognier, this one stands
out for its twang of grapefruit acidity.

8 **Vasse Felix Semillon/Sauvignon
Blanc 2009** £9.99
Brisk but not green, generous Bordeaux-type dry white
from Margaret River is full of life.

8 **Domäne Wachau Terraces
Grüner Veltliner 2009** £7.99
Fine mineral aperitif of obvious merit, it's lush and lively,
just off-dry.

8 **Virtue Sauvignon Blanc/Chardonnay 2009** £4.19
Easy-drinking, crowd-pleasing eco-wine.

6 **Chapel Down Flint Dry 2009** £7.69
Spare but not austere reasonably balanced dry appley
refresher, but unwarrantably expensive.

7 **Chapel Down Bacchus 2009** £9.49
Wasps' nest smell and an intriguing rhubarb note in the
dry, fresh fruit, but at the price you're being stung.

8 Cuvée Pêcheur 2009   **£3.99**
Eager but not green Toulouse vin de pays is a refreshing bargain.

8 Domaine de Plantérieu 2009   **£5.49**
Clean, balanced party white from Gascony is just 10.5% alcohol.

**8 Fief Guérin Vieilles Vignes
     Muscadet 2009**   **£6.49**
From posh-sounding AC Côtes de Grandlieu Sur Lie, this is a flinty, briny flavour-packed spin on the usually acid Muscadet theme, with a big hint of cock-a-leekie on the nose.

9 Saumur Les Andides 2009   **£6.99**
Fascinating balance of zing and ripe orchard fruit in this vigorous Loire Chenin Blanc with a waft of honeysuckle. A marvel at the price.

8 Cheverny Le Petit Salvard 2009   **£7.99**
Big bracing Loire Sauvignon with vegetal fruity and limey finish.

8 Vouvray Domaine de Vieux Vauvert 2008   **£7.99**
'Medium-dry' Loire Chenin Blanc is soft (not sweet) and seductive in its balance of ripeness and citrus edge. Fine aperitif.

**8 Dom Brial Muscat de
     Rivesaltes 2007 50cl**   **£8.49**
Poised, grapey vin doux naturel with 16% alcohol and luscious but controlled sweetness. Waitrose Direct.

**8 Bouchard Aîné et Fils
     White Burgundy 2008**   **£8.99**
Smartly packaged Mâcon/Côte d'Or blend has gold colour, apple-pie richness, crisp finish.

9 Menetou-Salon Domaine
Henry Pellé Vignes de Ratier 2008 £11.99
Lush Loire Sauvignon with a lick of richness from sur lie ageing has bold green orchard flavours to match saucy fish dishes.

8 Waitrose Sancerre la Franchotte 2009 £11.99
Richly coloured and nuanced pebbly-but-plump grand Loire Sauvignon by respected Joseph Mellot is good value by Sancerre standards.

10 Domaine Naudet Sancerre 2009 £12.49
Super stony Loire classic with zippy Sauvignon grassiness and a basketful of fruit. My Sancerre of the year.

9 Château Jolys Cuvée Jean 2007 £12.99
Golden-hued, Sauternes-style sweetie from Pyrenean AC Jurançon is honeyed but beautifully balanced. Great treat with foie gras.

9 Waitrose Sauternes 2006 37.5cl £13.49
Ambrosial pudding wine from legendary Château Suduiraut is superb now and will keep, and keep.

9 Vouvray Domaine Huet Le
Haut-Lieu Sec 2007 £18.49
Esoteric dry but lush Loire Chenin Blanc from a great biodynamic estate is at once luxurious and mineral. A glorious aperitif wine.

8 Kendermanns Special Edition
Riesling 2008 £5.99
From the people famed (notorious?) for the Black Tower brand, this is a different construct altogether, a brisk but ripe and long classic appley Rheinpfalz Riesling.

GERMANY

8 Dr Wagner Riesling 2009 £7.99
Light in weight and just 10% alcohol, this fine, slaty, racy
Moselle has a delectable honey note.

9 Dr Bassermann-Jordan Riesling 2008 £8.99
Lovely apple-strudel Rheinpfalz off-dry but crisp-finishing
classic Riesling with 10% alcohol.

8 Dönnhoff Kreuznacher Krötenpufl
Riesling Spätlese 2006 £18.99
From a biodynamic Nahe vineyard (Krötenpufl translates
as 'frog pond'), a lovely long sweet-apple, racy mature
wine just showing a petrolly nuance; 8% alcohol.

HUNGARY

8 Eva's Vineyard Chenin Blanc/Pinot
Grigio/Királyleányka 2009 £3.99
Pleasing honeyed autumn smell and friendly fresh fruit – a
sunny bargain.

ITALY

8 Vignale Pinot Grigio 2009 £4.89
Flowery-nosed fresh and friendly variation on the theme
has a touch of nectar to broaden its appeal.

10 Inycon Growers' Selection Fiano 2009 £6.49
Apples and pears, peaches and hazelnuts in the cornucopia
this dazzling Sicilian wine evokes. Bountiful, but dry and
upliftingly fresh. I believe the Fiano grape is the rightful
heir, should Pinot Grigio falter in popularity.

8 La Monacesca Verdicchio
di Matelica 2008 £9.99
Distinct from the usual Castelli di Jesi of the Marches,
this is a hefty vegetal dry wine of arresting intensity and
weight. Great food-matcher.

8 **Waitrose Sauvignon Blanc 2009** £8.79

Made by the ubiquitous Villa Maria, a brisk, briny and spangly Sauvignon in the authentic Kiwi tradition.

10 **The Ned Pinot Grigio 2009** £9.99

The excellent name is that of a high peak in the Waihopai Valley of Marlborough with the synonymous vineyard on its lower slopes. The wine is just the slightest shade pink, and the smoky, exotic orchardy fruit is beautifully extracted in the Alsace Pinot Gris style, with 14% alcohol. My Kiwi wine of the year.

9 **Seifried Estate Sweet Agnes**
Riesling Ice Wine 2008 £13.99

Amazing stickie from grapes picked frozen is a beautiful nectar at 10% alcohol. Is there anything the Kiwis can't do? Waitrose Direct.

7 **Cloudy Bay Te Koko**
Sauvignon Blanc 2007 £22.99

With an eye on the price, I thought I detected aromas of both coffee and toffee in this extraordinary oak-fermented millionaires' wine. Nice, though. Waitrose Direct.

8 **Arniston Bay Lighthouse Collection**
Chenin Blanc/Colombard 2009 £5.29

In spite of myself, I liked this mega-brand for being clean, brisk and not too sweet – and 10% alcohol.

8 **Springfield Estate Special Cuvée**
Sauvignon Blanc 2009 £9.39

Tart citrus acidity over copious asparagus fruit in this vivid wine for adult tastes.

8 **Ken Forrester The FMC**
Chenin Blanc 2008 £17.99

Super-ripe fruit salad (banana and sweet melon included) dry and impactful luxury wine with 14.5% alcohol is pricey, but its unique appeal outdoes plenty of overpriced white burgundies I can think of. Waitrose Direct.

NEW ZEALAND

SOUTH AFRICA

6 Torres Natureo 2009 £5.99

This is 'de-alcoholised' wine and as such I wouldn't dream of drinking it, but by the miserable standards of these products, this isn't bad; tastes something like a dry-ish Muscat grape-juice.

9 Viña Esmeralda 2009 £6.99

Perennial favourite from Torres is a dry but grapily aromatic Muscat-Gewürztraminer blend in the Alsace style, but lighter and very fresh.

8 Marqués de Murrieta Capellania
Reserva Rioja 2004 £17.49

Grand old unreconstructed white Rioja is gold, nutty-rich and apple-sweet with a whiff of petrol.

10 Wente Morning Fog Chardonnay 2008 £7.99

Not the most upbeat of names, but this sublime lush, plush gold-coloured creamy but apple-crisp de luxe dry Californian white (from the Livermore Valley south of San Francisco Bay) has all-weather appeal at what seems an inexplicably reasonable price. Is the secret the 3% Gewürztraminer in the blend?

SPAIN

USA

10 Sandeman Imperial Tawny Port £9.65

Silky, figgy, copper-ruby-coloured tawny easily mistakable for a ten-year-old has focused intensity of fruit, creamy toffee richness and clean edge (20% alcohol). Terrific quality and character for a port at this price. Biggest branches only or Waitrose Direct.

8 Henriques & Henriques Full Rich
3-Year-Old Madeira £11.49

Nice genteel sweet blend with fire-island char and lovely figgy-nutty fruit. Accessible, and can be chilled; 19% alcohol.

PORTUGAL

9 Blandy's Single Harvest Malmsey 2001 £14.99

A rare colheita (vintage-dated) Madeira of dark hue, roasted, toasted intense fruitcake flavours of almost austere purity as well as wicked richness and 19% alcohol. Just lovely and great value as an after-dinner drink. Biggest branches only or Waitrose Direct.

9 Blandy's Sercial 10-Year-Old Madeira 50cl £18.99

Bronze colour, orange-zest nose, dark near-burnt conserved fruit flavours, really quite dry. Fabulous to serve chilled; 19% alcohol. The Bual and Verdelho in this range are equally heavenly in their ways.

8 Ackerman Sparkling Cabernet Franc Rosé Brut £7.99

Delicately pink Loire fizz is bright with summer soft fruit and thoroughly convincing.

8 Charles Viénot Brut Royal £14.99

Not champagne but a 'vin mousseux de France' made by a family with Champagne connections. It has a zingy elderflower nose, distinctly champagne-like fruit and sparkle and works very well indeed.

8 Waitrose Special Reserve Vintage Champagne Brut 2002 £26.99

Affable mellow brioche style to this lovely mature vintage wine at a fair price.

8 Taittinger Prestige Brut Rosé £40.99

Frightfully expensive, but this elegant, non-vintage, pink champagne does deliver the most amazingly focused and wildly ebullient strawberry fruit – really remarkable.

ITALY

 SanLeo Prosecco £7.99

Positively yeasty and vigorously fizzy just-dry style with real charm and 11% alcohol. Stands out.

SPAIN

 Waitrose Cava Brut £6.99

Major improvement on the usual tinny cava style, this has a big apple smell and plenty of brisk fresh orchard fruit.

What wine
words mean

Wine labels are getting crowded. It's mostly thanks to the unending torrent of new regulation. Lately, for example, the European Union has decided that all wines sold within its borders must display a health warning: 'Contains Sulphites'. All wines are made with the aid of preparations containing sulphur to combat diseases in the vineyards and bacterial infections in the winery. You can't make wine without sulphur. Even 'organic' wines are made with it. But some people are sensitive to the traces of sulphur in some wines, so we must all be informed of the presence of this hazardous material.

That's the way it is. And it might not be long before some even sterner warnings will be added about another ingredient in wine. Alcohol is the new tobacco, as the regulators see it, and in the near future we can look forward to some stern admonishments about the effects of alcohol. In the meantime, the mandatory information on every label includes the quantity, alcoholic strength and country of origin, along with the name of the producer. The region will be specified, vaguely on wines from loosely regulated countries such as Australia, and precisely on wines from over-regulated countries such as France. Wines from 'classic' regions of Europe – Bordeaux, Chianti, Rioja and so on – are mostly labelled according to their location rather than their constituent grape varieties. If it says Sancerre, it's taken as read that you either know it's made with Sauvignon Blanc grapes, or don't care.

Wines from just about everywhere else make no such assumptions. If a New Zealand wine is made from Sauvignon Blanc grapes, you can be sure the label will say so. This does quite neatly represent the gulf between the two worlds of winemaking. In traditional European regions, it's the place, the vineyard, that mostly determines the character of the wines. The French call it terroir, to encapsulate not just the lie of the land and the soil conditions but the wild variations in the weather from year to year as well. The grapes are merely the medium through which the timeless mysteries of the deep earth are translated into the ineffable glories of the wine, adjusted annually according to the vagaries of climate, variable moods of the winemaker, and who knows what else.

In the less arcane vineyards of the New World, the grape is definitely king. In hot valleys such as the Barossa (South Australia) or the Maipo (Chile) valleys, climate is relatively predictable and the soil conditions are managed by irrigation. It's the fruit that counts, and the style of the wine is determined by the variety – soft, spicy Shiraz; peachy, yellow Chardonnay and so on.

The main purpose of this glossary is, consequently, to give short descriptions of the 'classic' wines, including the names of the grapes they are made from, and of the 70-odd distinct grape varieties that make most of the world's wines. As well as these very brief descriptions, I have included equally shortened summaries of the regions and appellations of the better-known wines, along with some of the local terms used to indicate style and alleged qualities.

Finally, I have tried to explain in simple and rational terms the peculiar words I use in trying to convey the characteristics of wines described. 'Delicious' might need no further qualification, but the likes of 'bouncy', 'green' and 'liquorous' probably do.

A

abboccato – Medium-dry white wine style. Italy, especially Orvieto.

AC – *See* Appellation d'Origine Contrôlée.

acidity – To be any good, every wine must have the right level of acidity. It gives wine the element of dryness or sharpness it needs to prevent cloying sweetness or dull wateriness. If there is too much acidity, wine tastes raw or acetic (vinegary). Winemakers strive to create balanced acidity – either by cleverly controlling the natural processes, or by adding sugar and acid to correct imbalances.

aftertaste – The flavour that lingers in the mouth after swallowing the wine.

Aglianico – Black grape variety of southern Italy. It has romantic associations. When the ancient Greeks first colonised Italy in the seventh century BC, it was with the prime purpose of planting it as a vineyard (the Greek name for Italy was *Oenotria* – land of cultivated vines). The name for the vines the Greeks brought with them was Ellenico (as in Hellas, Greece), from which Aglianico is the modern rendering. To return to the point, these ancient vines, especially in the arid volcanic landscapes of Basilicata and Cilento, produce excellent dark, earthy and highly distinctive wines. A name to look out for.

Agriculture biologique – On French wine labels, an indication that the wine has been made by organic methods.

Albariño – White grape variety of Spain that makes intriguingly perfumed fresh and spicy dry wines, especially in esteemed Rias Baixas region.

alcohol – The alcohol levels in wines are expressed in terms of alcohol by volume ('abv'), that is, the percentage of the volume of the wine that is common, or ethyl, alcohol. A typical wine at 12 per cent abv is thus 12 parts alcohol and, in effect, 88 parts fruit juice.

The question of how much alcohol we can drink without harming ourselves in the short or long term is an impossible one to answer, but there is more or less general agreement among scientists that small amounts of alcohol are good for us, even if the only evidence of this is actuarial – the fact that mortality statistics show teetotallers live significantly shorter lives than moderate drinkers. According to the Department of Health, there are 'safe limits' to the amount of alcohol we should drink weekly. These limits are measured in units of alcohol, with a small glass of wine taken to be one unit. Men are advised that 28 units a week is the most they can drink without risk to health, and for women (whose liver function differs from that of men because of metabolic differences) the figure is 21 units.

If you wish to measure your consumption closely, note that a standard 75 cl bottle of wine at 12 per cent alcohol contains 9 units. A bottle of German Moselle at 8 per cent alcohol has only 6 units, but a bottle of Australian Chardonnay at 14 per cent has 10.5.

Alentejo – Wine region of southern Portugal (immediately north of the Algarve), with a fast-improving reputation, especially for sappy, keen reds from local grape varieties including Aragones, Castelão and Trincadeira grapes.

Almansa – DO winemaking region of Spain inland from Alicante, making great-value red wines.

Alsace – France's easternmost wine-producing region lies between the Vosges Mountains and the River Rhine, with Germany beyond. These conditions make for the production of some of the world's most delicious and fascinating white wines, always sold under the name of their constituent grapes. Pinot Blanc is the most affordable – and is well worth looking out for. The 'noble' grape varieties of the region are Gewürztraminer, Muscat, Riesling and Tokay Pinot Gris and they are always made on a single-variety basis. The richest, most exotic wines are those from individual *grand cru* vineyards, which are named on the label. Some *vendange tardive* (late harvest) wines are made, but tend to be expensive. All the wines are sold in tall, slim green bottles known as flûtes that closely resemble those of the Mosel, and the names of producers and grape varieties are often German too, so it is widely assumed that Alsace wines are German in style, if not in nationality. But this is not the case in either particular. Alsace wines are dry and quite unique in character – and definitely French.

Amarone – Style of red wine made in Valpolicella, Italy. Specially selected grapes are held back from the harvest and stored for several months to dry them out. They are then pressed and fermented into a highly concentrated speciality dry wine. Amarone means 'bitter', describing the dry style of the flavour.

amontillado – *See* sherry.

aperitif – If a wine is thus described, I believe it will give more pleasure before a meal than with one. Crisp, low-alcohol German wines and other delicately flavoured whites (including many dry Italians) are examples.

Appellation d'Origine Contrôlée – Commonly abbreviated to AC or AOC, this is the system under which quality wines are defined in France. About a third of the country's vast annual output qualifies, and there are more than 400 distinct AC zones. The declaration of an AC on the label signifies that the wine meets standards concerning location of vineyards and wineries, grape varieties and limits on harvest per hectare, methods of cultivation and vinification, and alcohol content. Wines are inspected and tasted by state-appointed committees. The one major aspect of any given wine that an AC cannot guarantee is that you will like it – but it certainly improves the chances.

Apulia – Anglicised name for Puglia.

Ardèche – Region of southern France to the west of the Rhône valley, home to a good vin de pays zone known as the Coteaux de L'Ardèche. Lots of decent-value reds from Syrah grapes, and some, less interesting, dry whites.

Assyrtiko – White grape variety of Greece now commonly named on dry white wines, sometimes of great quality, from the mainland and islands.

Asti – Town and major winemaking centre in Piedmont, Italy. The sparkling (spumante) sweet wines made from Moscato grapes are inexpensive and often delicious. Typical alcohol level is a modest 5 to 7 per cent.

attack – In wine tasting, the first impression made by the wine in the mouth.

Auslese – German wine-quality designation. *See* QmP.

B

Baga – Black grape variety indigenous to Portugal. Makes famously concentrated, juicy reds that get their deep colour from the grape's particularly thick skins. Look out for this name, now quite frequently quoted as the varietal on Portuguese wine labels. Often very good value for money.

balance – A big word in the vocabulary of wine tasting. Respectable wine must get two key things right: lots of fruitiness from the sweet grape juice, and plenty of acidity so the sweetness is 'balanced' with the crispness familiar in good dry whites and the dryness that marks out good reds. Some wines are noticeably 'well balanced' in that they have memorable fruitiness and the clean, satisfying 'finish' (last flavour in the mouth) that ideal acidity imparts.

Barbera – Black grape variety originally of Piedmont in Italy. Most commonly seen as Barbera d'Asti, the vigorously fruity red wine made around Asti – once better known for sweet sparkling Asti Spumante. Barbera grapes are now being grown in South America, often producing a sleeker, smoother style than at home in Italy.

Bardolino – Once fashionable, light red wine DOC of Veneto, north-west Italy. Bardolino is made principally from Corvina Veronese grapes plus Rondinella, Molinara and Negrara. Best wines are supposed to be those labelled *classico*, and *superiore* is applied to those aged a year and having at least 11.5 per cent alcohol.

Barossa Valley – Famed vineyard region north of Adelaide, Australia, produces hearty reds principally from Shiraz, Cabernet Sauvignon and Grenache grapes, plus plenty of lush white wine from Chardonnay. Also known for limey, long-lived, mineral dry whites from Riesling grapes.

barrique – Barrel in French. *En barrique* on a wine label signifies the wine has been matured in oak.

Beaujolais – Unique red wines from the southern reaches of Burgundy, France, are made from Gamay grapes. Beaujolais nouveau, now deeply unfashionable, provides a friendly introduction to the bouncy, red-fruit style of the wine, but for the authentic experience, go for Beaujolais Villages, from the region's better, northern vineyards. There are ten AC zones within this northern sector making wines under their own names. Known as the crus, these are Brouilly, Chénas, Chiroubles, Côte de Brouilly, Fleurie, Juliénas, Morgon, Moulin à Vent, Regnié and St Amour and produce most of the best wines of the region. Prices are higher than those for Beaujolais Villages, but by no means always justifiably so.

Beaumes de Venise – Village near Châteauneuf du Pape in France's Rhône valley, famous for sweet and alcoholic wine from Muscat grapes. Delicious, grapey wines. A small number of growers also make strong (sometimes rather tough) red wines under the village name.

Beaune – One of the two winemaking centres (the other is Nuits St Georges) at the heart of Burgundy in France. Three of the region's humbler appellations take the name of the town: Côtes de Beaune, Côtes de Beaune Villages and Hautes Côtes de Beaune. Wines made under these ACs are often, but by no means always, good value for money.

berry fruit – Some red wines deliver a burst of flavour in the mouth that corresponds to biting into a newly picked berry – strawberry, blackberry, etc. So a wine described as having berry fruit (by this writer, anyway) has freshness, liveliness, immediate appeal.

bianco – White wine, Italy.

Bical – White grape variety principally of Dão region of northern Portugal. Not usually identified on labels, because most of it goes into inexpensive sparkling wines. Can make still wines of very refreshing crispness.

biodynamics – A cultivation method taking the organic approach several steps further. Biodynamic winemakers plant and tend their vineyards according to a date and time calendar 'in harmony' with the movements of the planets. Some of France's best-known wine estates subscribe, and many more are going that way. It might all sound bonkers, but it's salutary to learn that biodynamics is based on principles first described by a very eminent man, the Austrian educationist Rudolph Steiner. He's lately been in the news for having written, in 1919, that farmers crazy enough to feed animal products to cattle would drive the livestock 'mad'.

bite – In wine tasting, the impression on the palate of a wine with plenty of acidity and, often, tannin.

blanc – White wine, France.

blanc de blancs – White wine from white grapes, France. May seem to be stating the obvious, but some white wines (e.g. champagne) are made, partially or entirely, from black grapes.

blanc de noirs – White wine from black grapes, France. Usually sparkling (especially champagne) made from black Pinot Meunier and Pinot Noir grapes, with no Chardonnay or other white varieties.

blanco – White wine, Spain and Portugal.

Blauer Zweigelt – Black grape variety of Austria, making a large proportion of the country's red wines, some of excellent quality.

Bobal – Black grape variety mostly of south-eastern Spain. Thick skin is good for colour and juice contributes acidity to blends.

bodega – In Spain, a wine producer or wine shop.

Bonarda – Black grape variety of northern Italy. Now more widely planted in Argentina, where it makes rather elegant red wines, often representing great value.

botrytis – Full name, *botrytis cinerea*, is that of a beneficent fungus that can attack ripe grape bunches late in the season, shrivelling the berries to a gruesome-looking mess, which yields concentrated juice of prized sweetness. Cheerfully known as 'noble rot', this fungus is actively encouraged by winemakers in regions as diverse as Sauternes (in Bordeaux), Monbazillac (in Bergerac), the Rhine and Mosel valleys and South Australia to make ambrosial dessert wines.

bouncy – The feel in the mouth of a red wine with young, juicy fruitiness. Good Beaujolais is bouncy, as are many north-west-Italian wines from Barbera and Dolcetto grapes.

Bourgogne Grand Ordinaire – Appellation of France's Burgundy region for 'ordinary' red wines from either Gamay or Pinot Noir grapes, or both. Some good-value wines, especially from the Buxy co-operative in the southern Chalonnais area.

Bourgueil – Appellation of Loire Valley, France. Long-lived red wines from Cabernet Franc grapes.

briary – In wine-tasting, associated with the flavours of fruit from prickly bushes such as blackberries.

brûlé – Pleasant burnt-toffee taste or smell, as in crème brûlée.

brut – Driest style of sparkling wine. Originally French, for very dry champagnes specially developed for the British market, but now used for sparkling wines from all round the world.

Buzet – Little-seen AC of south-west France overshadowed by Bordeaux but producing some characterful ripe reds.

C

Cabardès – Recent AC (1998) for red and rosé wines from area north of Carcassonne, Aude, France. Principally Cabernet Sauvignon and Merlot grapes.

Cabernet Franc – Black grape variety originally of France. It makes the light-bodied and keenly-edged red wines of the Loire Valley – such as Chinon and Saumur. And it is much grown in Bordeaux, especially in the appellation of St Emilion. Also now planted in Argentina, Australia and North America. Wines, especially in the Loire, are characterised by a leafy, sappy style and bold fruitiness. Most are best enjoyed young.

Cabernet Sauvignon – Black (or, rather, blue) grape variety now grown in virtually every wine-producing nation. When perfectly ripened, the grapes are smaller than many other varieties and have particularly thick skins. This means that when pressed, Cabernet grapes have a high proportion of skin to juice – and that makes for wine with lots of colour and tannin. In Bordeaux, the grape's traditional home, the grandest Cabernet-based wines have always been known as *vins de garde* (wines to keep) because they take years, even decades, to evolve as the effect of all that skin extraction preserves the fruit all the way to magnificent maturity. But in today's impatient world, these grapes are exploited in modern winemaking techniques to produce the sublime flavours of mature Cabernet without having to hang around for lengthy periods awaiting maturation. While there's nothing like a fine, ten-year-old claret (and nothing quite as expensive), there are many excellent Cabernets from around the world that amply illustrate this grape's characteristics. Classic smells and flavours include blackcurrants, cedar wood, chocolate, tobacco – even violets.

Cahors – An AC of the Lot Valley in south-west France once famous for 'black wine'. This was a curious concoction of straightforward wine mixed with a soupy must, made by boiling up new-pressed juice to concentrate it (through evaporation) before fermentation. The myth is still perpetuated that Cahors wine continues to be made in this way, but production on this basis actually ceased 150 years ago. Cahors today is no stronger, or blacker, than the wines of neighbouring appellations.

Cairanne – Village of the appellation collectively known as the Côtes du Rhône Villages in southern France. Cairanne is one of several villages entitled to put their name on the labels of wines made within their AC boundary, and the appearance of this name is quite reliably an indicator of a very good wine indeed.

Calatayud – DO (quality wine zone) near Zaragoza in the Aragon region of northern Spain where they're making some astonishingly good wines at bargain prices, mainly reds from Garnacha and Tempranillo grapes. These are the varieties that go into the light and oaky wines of Rioja, but in Calatayud, the wines are dark, dense and decidedly different.

Cannonau – Black grape native to Sardinia by name, but in fact the same variety as the ubiquitous Grenache of France (and Garnacha of Spain).

cantina sociale – *See* Co-op.

Carignan – Black grape variety of Mediterranean France. It is rarely identified on labels, but is a major constituent of wines from the southern Rhône and Languedoc-Roussillon regions. Known as Carignano in Italy and Cariñena in Spain.

Cariñena – A region of north-east Spain, south of Navarra, known for substantial reds, as well as the Spanish name for the Carignan grape *(qv)*.

Carmenère – Black grape variety once widely grown in Bordeaux but abandoned due to cultivation problems. Lately revived in South America where it is producing fine wines, sometimes with echoes of Bordeaux.

cassis – As a tasting note, signifies a wine that has a noticeable blackcurrant-concentrate flavour or smell. Much associated with the Cabernet Sauvignon grape.

Castelao – Portuguese black grape variety. Same as Periquita.

Catarratto – White grape variety of Sicily. In skilled hands it can make anything from keen, green-fruit dry whites to lush, oaked super-ripe styles. Also used for Marsala.

cat's pee – In tasting notes, a mildly jocular reference to a certain style of Sauvignon Blanc wine.

cava – The sparkling wine of Spain. Most originates in Catalonia, but the Denominación de Origen (DO) guarantee of authenticity is open to producers in many regions of the country. Much cava is very reasonably priced even though it is made by the same method as champagne – second fermentation in bottle, known in Spain as the *método clásico*.

CdR – Côtes du Rhône.

Cépage – Grape variety, French. 'Cépage Merlot' on a label simply means the wine is made largely or exclusively from Merlot grapes.

Chablis – Northernmost AC of France's Burgundy region. Its dry white wines from Chardonnay grapes are known for their fresh and steely style, but the best wines also age very gracefully into complex classics.

Chambourcin – Sounds like a cream cheese but it's a relatively modern (1963) French hybrid black grape that makes some good non-appellation lightweight-but-concentrated reds in the Loire Valley and now some heftier versions in Australia.

Chardonnay – The world's most popular grape variety. Said to originate from the village of Chardonnay in the Mâconnais region of southern Burgundy, the vine is now planted in every wine-producing nation. Wines are commonly characterised by generous colour and sweet-apple smell, but styles range from lean and sharp to opulently rich. Australia started the craze for oaked Chardonnay, the gold-coloured, super-ripe, buttery 'upfront' wines that are a caricature of lavish and outrageously expensive burgundies such as Meursault and Puligny-Montrachet. Rich to the point of egginess, these Aussie pretenders are now giving way to a sleeker, more minerally style with much less oak presence – if any at all. California and Chile, New Zealand and South Africa are competing hard to imitate the Burgundian style, and Australia's success in doing so.

Châteauneuf du Pape – Famed appellation centred on a picturesque village of the southern Rhône valley in France where in the 1320s French Pope Clement V had a splendid new château built for himself as a country retreat amidst his vineyards. The red wines of the AC, which can be made from 13 different grape varieties but principally Grenache, Syrah and Mourvèdre, are regarded as the best of the southern Rhône and have become rather expensive – but they can be sensationally good. Expensive white wines are also made.

Chenin blanc – White grape variety of the Loire Valley, France. Now also grown farther afield, especially in South Africa. Makes dry, soft white wines and also rich, sweet styles. Sadly, many low-cost Chenin wines are bland and uninteresting.

cherry – In wine tasting, either a pale red colour or, more commonly, a smell or flavour akin to the sun-warmed, bursting sweet ripeness of cherries. Many Italian wines, from lightweights such as Bardolino and Valpolicella to serious Chianti, have this character. 'Black cherry' as a description is often used of Merlot wines – meaning they are sweet but have a firmness associated with the thicker skins of black cherries.

Cinsault – Black grape variety of southern France, where it is invariably blended with others in wines of all qualities ranging from vin de pays to the pricy reds of Châteauneuf du Pape. Also much planted in South Africa. The effect in wine is to add keen aromas (sometimes compared with turpentine!) and softness to the blend. The name is often spelt Cinsaut.

Clape, La – A small cru (defined quality-vineyard area) within the Coteaux du Languedoc where the growers make some seriously delicious red wines, mainly from Carignan, Grenache and Syrah grapes. A name worth looking out for on labels from the region.

claret – The red wine of Bordeaux, France. It comes from Latin clarus, meaning 'clear', recalling a time when the red wines of the region were much lighter in colour than they are now.

clarete – On Spanish labels indicates a pale-coloured red wine. Tinto signifies a deeper hue.

classed growth – English translation of French *cru classé* describes a group of 60 individual wine estates in the Médoc district of Bordeaux, which in 1855 were granted this new status on the basis that their wines were the most expensive at that time. The classification was a promotional wheeze to attract attention to the Bordeaux stand at that year's Great Exhibition in Paris. Amazingly, all of the 60 wines concerned are still in production and most still occupy more or less their original places in the pecking order price-wise. The league was divided up into five divisions from Premier Grand Cru Classé (just four wines originally, with one promoted in 1971 – the only change ever made to the classification) to Cinquième Grand Cru Classé. Other regions of Bordeaux, notably Graves and St Emilion, have since imitated Médoc and introduced their own rankings of *cru classé* estates.

classic – An overused term in every respect – wine descriptions being no exception. In this book, the word is used to describe a very good wine of its type. So, a 'classic' Cabernet Sauvignon is one that is recognisably and admirably characteristic of that grape.

Classico – Under Italy's wine laws, this word appended to the name of a DOC zone has an important significance. The classico wines of the region can only be made from vineyards lying in the best-rated areas, and wines thus labelled (e.g. Chianti Classico, Soave Classico, Valpolicella Classico) can be reliably counted on to be a cut above the rest.

Colombard – White grape variety of southern France. Once employed almost entirely for making the wine that is distilled for armagnac and cognac brandies, but lately restored to varietal prominence in the Vin de Pays des Côtes de Gascogne where high-tech wineries turn it into a fresh and crisp, if unchallenging, dry wine at a budget price. But beware, cheap Colombard (especially from South Africa) can still be very dull.

Conca de Barbera – Winemaking region of Catalonia, Spain.

co-op – Very many of France's good-quality, inexpensive wines are made by co-operatives. These are wine-producing factories whose members, and joint-owners, are local *vignerons* (vine growers). Each year they sell their harvests to the co-op for turning into branded wines. In Italy, co-op wines can be identified by the words *Cantina Sociale* on the label and in Germany by the term *Winzergenossenschaft*.

Corbières – A name to look out for. It's an AC of France's Midi (deep south) and produces countless robust reds and a few interesting whites, often at bargain prices.

Cortese – White grape variety of Piedmont, Italy. At its best, makes amazingly delicious, keenly brisk and fascinating wines, including those of the Gavi DOCG. Worth seeking out.

Costières de Nîmes – Until 1989, this AC of southern France was known as the Costières de Gard. It forms a buffer between the southern Rhône and Languedoc-Roussillon regions, and makes wines from broadly the same range of grape varieties. It's a name to look out for, the best red wines being notable for their concentration of colour and fruit, with the earthy-spiciness of the better Rhône wines and a likeable liquorice note. A few good white wines, too, and even a decent rosé or two.

Côte – In French, it simply means a side, or slope, of a hill. The implication in wine terms is that the grapes come from a vineyard ideally situated for maximum sunlight, good drainage and the unique soil conditions prevailing on the hill in question. It's fair enough to claim that vines grown on slopes might get more sunlight than those grown on the flat, but there is no guarantee whatsoever that any wine labelled 'Côtes du' this or that is made from grapes grown on a hillside anyway. Côtes du Rhône wines are a case in point. Many 'Côtes' wines come from entirely level vineyards and it is worth remembering that many of the vineyards of Bordeaux, producing most of the world's priciest wines, are little short of prairie-flat. The quality factor is determined much more significantly by the weather and the talents of the winemaker.

Côtes de Blaye – Appellation Contrôlée zone of Bordeaux on the right bank of the River Gironde, opposite the more prestigious Médoc zone of the left bank. Best-rated vinyards qualify for the AC Premières Côtes de Blaye. A couple of centuries ago, Blaye (pronounced 'bligh') was the grander of the two, and even today makes some wines that compete well for quality, and at a fraction of the price of wines from its more fashionable rival across the water.

Côtes de Bourg – AC neighbouring Côtes de Blaye, making red wines of fast-improving quality and value.

Côtes du Luberon – Appellation Contrôlée zone of Provence in south-east France. Wines, mostly red, are similar in style to Côtes du Rhône.

Côtes du Rhône – One of the biggest and best-known appellations of south-east France, covering an area roughly defined by the southern reaches of the valley of the River Rhône. Long notorious for cheap and execrable reds, the Côtes du Rhône AC has lately achieved remarkable improvements in quality at all points along the price scale. Lots of brilliant-value warm and spicy reds, principally from Grenache and Syrah grapes. There are also some white and rosé wines.

Côtes du Rhône Villages – Appellation within the larger Côtes du Rhône AC for wine of supposed superiority made in a number of zones associated with a long list of nominated individual villages.

Côtes du Roussillon – Huge appellation of south-west France known for strong, dark, peppery reds often offering very decent value.

Côtes du Roussillon Villages – Appellation for superior wines from a number of nominated locations within the larger Roussillon AC. Some of these village wines can be of exceptional quality and value.

crianza – Means 'nursery' in Spanish. On Rioja and Navarra wines, the designation signifies a wine that has been nursed through a maturing period of at least a year in oak casks and a further six months in bottle before being released for sale.

cru – A word that crops up with confusing regularity on French wine labels. It means 'the growing' or 'the making' of a wine and asserts that the wine concerned is from a specific vineyard. Under the Appellation Contrôlée rules, countless crus are classified in various hierarchical ranks. Hundreds of individual vineyards are described as premier cru or grand cru in the classic wine regions of Alsace, Bordeaux, Burgundy and Champagne. The common denominator is that the wine can be counted on to be enormously expensive. On humbler wines, the use of the word cru tends to be mere decoration.

cru classé – *See* classed growth.

cuve – A vat for wine. French.

cuvée – French for the wine in a cuve, or vat. The word is much used on labels to imply that the wine is from just one vat, and thus of unique, unblended character. Première cuvée is supposedly the best wine from a given pressing because the grapes have had only the initial, gentle squashing to extract the free-run juice. Subsequent cuvées will have been from harsher pressings, grinding the grape pulp to extract the last drop of juice.

D

Dão – Major wine-producing region of northern Portugal now turning out much more interesting reds than it used to – worth looking out for anything made by mega-producer Sogrape.

demi sec – 'Half-dry' style of French (and some other) wines. Beware. It can mean anything from off-dry to cloyingly sweet.

DO – Denominación de Origen, Spain's wine-regulating scheme, similar to France's AC, but older – the first DO region was Rioja, from 1926. DO wines are Spain's best, accounting for a third of the nation's annual production.

DOC – Stands for Denominazione di Origine Controllata, Italy's equivalent of France's AC. The wines are made according to the stipulations of each of its 280 denominated zones of origin, a number now approaching 50, of which enjoy the superior classification of DOCG (DOC with *e Garantita* – guaranteed – appended).

Durif – Rare black grape variety mostly of California, where it is also known as Petite Sirah, but with some plantings in Australia.

E

earthy – A tricky word in the wine vocabulary. In this book, its use is meant to be complimentary. It indicates that the wine somehow suggests the soil the grapes were grown in, even (perhaps a shade too poetically) the landscape in which the vineyards lie. The amazing-value red wines of the torrid, volcanic southernmost regions of Italy are often described as earthy. This is an association with the pleasantly 'scorched' back-flavour in wines made from the ultra-ripe harvests of this near-sub-tropical part of the world.

edge – A wine with edge is one with evident (although not excessive) acidity.

élevé – 'Brought up' in French. Much used on wine labels where the wine has been matured (brought up) in oak barrels, *élevé en fûts de chêne*, to give it extra dimensions.

Entre Deux Mers – Meaning 'between two seas', it's a region lying between the Dordogne and Garonne rivers of Bordeaux, now mainly known for dry white wines from Sauvignon and Semillon grapes.

Estremadura – Wine-producing region occupying Portugal's coastal area north of Lisbon. Lots of interesting wines from indigenous grape varieties, usually at bargain prices. If a label mentions Estremadura, it is a safe rule that there might be something good within.

F

Faugères – AC of the Languedoc in south-west France. Source of many hearty, economic reds.

Feteasca – White grape variety widely grown in Romania. Name means 'maiden's grape' and the wine tends to be soft and slightly sweet.

Fiano – White grape variety of the Campania of southern Italy and Sicily, lately revived. It is said to have been cultivated by the ancient Romans for a wine called Apianum.

finish – The last flavour lingering in the mouth after wine has been swallowed.

fino – Pale and very dry style of sherry. You drink it thoroughly chilled – and you don't keep it any longer after opening than other dry white wines. Needs to be fresh to be at its best.

Fitou – One of the first 'designer' wines, it's an appellation in France's Languedoc region, where production is dominated by one huge co-operative, the Vignerons de Mont Tauch. Back in the 1970s, this co-op paid a corporate-image company to come up with a Fitou logo and label-design style, and the wines have prospered ever since. And it's not just packaging – Fitou at all price levels can be very good value, especially from the Mont Tauch co-op.

flabby – Fun word describing a wine that tastes dilute or watery, with insufficient acidity.

fruit – In tasting terms, the fruit is the greater part of the overall flavour of a wine. The wine is (or should be) after all, composed entirely of fruit.

G

Gamay – The black grape that makes all red Beaujolais and some ordinary burgundy. It is a pretty safe rule to avoid Gamay wines from any other region, but there are exceptions.

Garganega – White grape variety of the Veneto region of north-east Italy. Best known as the principal ingredient of Soave, but occasionally included in varietal blends and mentioned as such on labels. Correctly pronounced 'gar-GAN-iga'.

Garnacha – Spanish black grape variety synonymous with Grenache of France. It is blended with Tempranillo to make the red wines of Rioja and Navarra, and is now quite widely cultivated elsewhere in Spain to make grippingly fruity varietals.

garrigue – Arid land of France's deep south giving its name to a style of red wine that notionally evokes the herby, heated, peppery flavours associated with such a landscape. A tricky metaphor!

Gavi – DOCG for dry but rich white wine from Cortese grapes in Piedmont, north-west Italy. Trendy Gavi di Gavi wines tend to be enjoyably lush, but are rather expensive.

Gewürztraminer – One of the great grape varieties of Alsace, France. At their best, the wines are perfumed with lychees and are richly, spicily fruity, yet quite dry. Gewürztraminer from Alsace is almost always relatively expensive, but the grape is also grown with some success in Eastern Europe, Germany, Italy and South America, and sold at more approachable prices. Pronounced 'ge-VOORTS-traminner'.

Givry – AC for red and white wines in the Côte Chalonnaise sub-region of Burgundy. Source of some wonderfully natural-tasting reds that might be lighter than those of the more prestigious Côte d'Or to the north, but have great merits of their own. Relatively, the wines are often underpriced.

Graciano – Black grape variety of Spain that is one of the minor constituents of Rioja. Better known in its own right in Australia where it can make dense, spicy, long-lived red wines.

green – I don't often use this in the pejorative. Green, to me, is a likeable degree of freshness, especially in Sauvignon Blanc wines.

Grenache – The mainstay of the wines of the southern Rhône Valley in France. Grenache is usually the greater part of the mix in Côtes du Rhône reds and is widely planted right across the neighbouring Languedoc-Roussillon region. It's a big-cropping variety that thrives even in the hottest climates and is really a blending grape – most commonly with Syrah, the noble variety of the northern Rhône. Few French wines are labelled with its name, but the grape has caught on in Australia in a big way and it is now becoming a familiar varietal, known for strong, dark liquorous reds. Grenache is the French name for what is originally a Spanish variety, Garnacha.

Grillo – White grape of Sicily said to be among the island's oldest indigenous varieties, pre-dating the arrival of the Greeks in 600 BC. Much used for fortified Marsala, it has lately been revived for interesting, aromatic dry table wines.

grip – In wine-tasting terminology, the sensation in the mouth produced by a wine that has a healthy quantity of tannin in it. A wine with grip is a good wine. A wine with too much tannin, or which is still too young (the tannin hasn't 'softened' with age) is not described as having grip, but as mouth-puckering – or simply undrinkable.

Grolleau – Black grape variety of the Loire Valley principally cultivated for Rosé d'Anjou.

Grüner Veltliner – The 'national' white-wine grape of Austria. In the past it made mostly soft, German-style everyday wines, but now is behind some excellent dry styles, too.

H

halbtrocken – 'Half-dry' in Germany's wine vocabulary. A reassurance that the wine is not some ghastly sugared Liebfraumilch-style confection.

hock – The wine of Germany's Rhine river valleys. Traditionally, but no longer consistently, it comes in brown bottles, as distinct from the wine of the Mosel river valleys – which comes in green ones.

I

Indicazione Geografica Tipica – Italy's recently instituted wine-quality designation, broadly equivalent to France's vin de pays. The label has to state the geographical location of the vineyard and will often (but not always) state the principal grape varieties from which the wine is made.

J

jammy – The 'sweetness' in dry red wines is supposed to evoke ripeness rather than sugariness. Sometimes, flavours include a sweetness reminiscent of jam. Usually a fault in the winemaking technique.

joven – Young wine, Spanish. In regions such as Rioja, vino joven is a synonym for sin crianza, which means 'without ageing' in cask or bottle.

K

Kabinett – Under Germany's bewildering wine-quality rules, this is a classification of a top-quality (QmP) wine. Expect a keen, dry, racy style. The name comes from the cabinet or cupboard in which winemakers traditionally kept their most treasured bottles.

Kekfrankos – Black grape variety of Hungary, particularly the Sopron region, which makes some of the country's more interesting red wines, characterised by colour and spiciness. Same variety as Austria's Blaufrankisch.

L

Ladoix – Unfashionable AC at northern edge of Côtes de Beaune makes some of Burgundy's true bargain reds. A name to look out for.

Lambrusco – The name is that of a black grape variety widely grown across northern Italy. True Lambrusco wine is red, dry and very slightly sparkling, but from the 1980s Britain has been deluged with a strange, sweet manifestation of the style, which has done little to enhance the good name of the original. Good Lambrusco is delicious and fun, but in this country now very hard to find. See section for Booths.

Languedoc-Roussillon – Vast area of southern France, including the country's south-west Mediterranean region. The source, now, of many great-value wines from countless ACs and vin de pays zones.

legs – The liquid residue left clinging to the sides of the glass after wine has been swirled. The persistence of the legs is an indicator of the weight of alcohol. Also known as 'tears'.

lieu dit – This is starting to appear on French wine labels. It translates as an 'agreed place' and is an area of vineyard defined as of particular character or merit, but not classified under wine law. Usually, the lieu dit's name is stated, with the implication that the wine in question has special value.

liquorice – The pungent slightly burnt flavours of this once-fashionable confection are detectable in some wines made from very ripe grapes, for example, the Malbec harvested in Argentina and several varieties grown in the very hot vineyards of southernmost Italy. A close synonym is 'tarry'. This characteristic is by no means a fault in red wine, unless very dominant, but it can make for a challenging flavour that might not appeal to all tastes.

liquorous – Wines of great weight and glyceriney texture (evidenced by the 'legs', or 'tears', which cling to the glass after the wine has been swirled) are always noteworthy. The connection with liquor is drawn in respect of the feel of the wine in the mouth, rather than with the higher alcoholic strength of spirits.

Lugana – DOC of Lombardy, Italy known for a dry white wine that is often of real distinction – rich, almondy stuff from the ubiquitous Trebbiano grape.

M

Macabeo – One of the main grapes used for cava, the sparkling wine of Spain. It is the same grape as Viura.

Mâcon – Town and collective appellation of southern Burgundy, France. Lightweight white wines from Chardonnay grapes and similarly light reds from Pinot Noir and some Gamay. The better ones, and the ones exported, have the AC Mâcon-Villages and there are individual village wines with their own ACs including Mâcon-Clessé, Mâcon-Viré and Mâcon-Lugny.

Malbec – Black grape variety grown on a small scale in Bordeaux, and the mainstay of the wines of Cahors in France's Dordogne region under the name Cot. Now much better known for producing big butch reds in Argentina.

Manzanilla – Pale, very dry sherry of Sanlucar de Barrameda, a resort town on the Bay of Cadiz in Spain. Manzanilla is proud to be distinct from the pale, very dry fino sherry of the main producing town of Jerez de la Frontera an hour's drive inland. Drink it chilled and fresh – it goes downhill in an opened bottle after just a few days, even if kept (as it should be) in the fridge.

Margaret River – Vineyard region of Western Australia regarded as ideal for grape varieties including Cabernet Sauvignon. It has a relatively cool climate and a reputation for making sophisticated wines, both red and white.

Marlborough – Best-known vineyard region of New Zealand's South Island has a cool climate and a name for brisk but cerebral Sauvignon Blanc and Chardonnay wines.

Marsanne – White grape variety of the northern Rhône Valley and, increasingly, of the wider south of France. It's known for making well-coloured wines with heady aroma and fruit.

Mataro – Black grape variety of Australia. It's the same as the Mourvèdre of France and Monastrell of Spain.

McLaren Vale – Vineyard region south of Adelaide in south-east Australia. Known for blockbuster Shiraz (and Chardonnay) that can be of great balance and quality from winemakers who keep the ripeness under control.

meaty – Weighty, rich red wine style.

Mendoza – The region to watch in Argentina. Lying to the east of the Andes mountains, just about opposite the best vineyards of Chile on the other side, Mendoza accounts for the bulk of Argentine wine production, with quality improving fast.

Merlot – One of the great black wine grapes of Bordeaux, and now grown all over the world. The name is said to derive from the French merle, meaning a blackbird. Characteristics of Merlot-based wines attract descriptions such as 'plummy' and 'plump' with black-cherry aroma. The grapes are larger than most, and thus have less skin in proportion to their flesh. This means the resulting wines have less tannin than wines from smaller-berry varieties such as Cabernet Sauvignon, and are therefore, in the Bordeaux context at least, more suitable for drinking while still relatively young.

middle palate – In wine-tasting, the impression given by the wine when it is held in the mouth.

Midi – Catch-all term for the deep south of France west of the Rhône Valley.

mineral – Good dry white wines can have a crispness and freshness that somehow evokes this word. Purity of flavour is a key.

Minervois – AC for (mostly) red wines from vineyards around the town of Minerve in the Languedoc-Roussillon region of France. Often good value. The new Minervois La Livinière AC – a sort of Minervois Grand Cru – is host to some great estates including Château Maris and Vignobles Lorgeril.

Monastrell – Black grape variety of Spain, widely planted in Mediterranean regions for inexpensive wines notable for their high alcohol and toughness – though they can mature into excellent, soft reds. The variety is known in France as Mourvèdre and in Australia as Mataro.

Monbazillac – AC for sweet, dessert wines within the wider appellation of Bergerac in south-west France. Made from the same grape varieties (principally Sauvignon and Semillon) that go into the much costlier counterpart wines of Barsac and Sauternes near Bordeaux, these stickies from botrytis-affected, late-harvested grapes can be delicious and good value for money.

Montalcino – Hill town of Tuscany, Italy, and a DOCG for strong and very long-lived red wines from Brunello grapes. The wines are mostly very expensive. Rosso di Montalcino, a DOC for the humbler wines of the zone, is often a good buy.

Montepulciano – Black grape variety of Italy. Best known in Montepulciano d'Abruzzo, the juicy, purply-black and bramble-fruited red of the Abruzzi region midway down Italy's Adriatic side. Also the grape in the rightly popular hearty reds of Rosso Conero from around Ancona in the Marches. Not to be confused with the hill town of Montepulciano in Tuscany, famous for expensive Vino Nobile di Montepulciano wine.

morello – Lots of red wines have smells and flavours redolent of cherries. Morello cherries, among the darkest coloured and sweetest of all varieties and the preferred choice of cherry-brandy producers, have a distinct sweetness resembled by some wines made from Merlot grapes. A morello whiff or taste is generally very welcome.

Moscatel – Spanish Muscat.

Moscato – *See* Muscat.

Moselle – The wine of Germany's Mosel river valleys, collectively known for winemaking purposes as Mosel-Saar-Ruwer. The wine always comes in slim, green bottles, as distinct from the brown bottles traditionally, but no longer exclusively, employed for Rhine wines.

Mourvèdre – Widely planted black grape variety of southern France. It's an ingredient in many of the wines of Provence, the Rhône and Languedoc, including the ubiquitous vin de pays d'Oc. It's a hot-climate vine and the wine is usually blended with other varieties to give sweet aromas and 'backbone' to the mix. Known as Mataro in Australia and Monastrell in Spain.

Muscadet – One of France's most familiar everyday whites, made from a grape called the Melon or Melon de Bourgogne. It comes from vineyards at the estuarial end of the River Loire, and has a sea-breezy freshness about it. The better wines are reckoned to be those from the vineyards in the Sèvre et Maine region, and many are made sur lie – 'on the lees' – meaning that the wine is left in contact with the yeasty deposit of its fermentation until just before bottling, in an endeavour to add interest to what can sometimes be an acidic and fruitless style.

Muscat – Grape variety with origins in ancient Greece, and still grown widely among the Aegean islands for the production of sweet white wines. Muscats are the wines that taste more like grape juice than any other – but the high sugar levels ensure they are also among the most alcoholic of wines, too. Known as Moscato in Italy, the grape is much used for making sweet sparkling wines, as in Asti Spumante or Moscato d'Asti. There are several appellations in south-west France for inexpensive Muscats made rather like port, part-fermented before the addition of grape alcohol to halt the conversion of sugar into alcohol, creating a sweet and heady vin doux naturel. Dry Muscat wines, when well made, have a delicious sweet aroma but a refreshing, light touch with flavours reminiscent variously of orange blossom, wood smoke and grapefruit.

must – New-pressed grape juice prior to fermentation.

N

Navarra – DO wine-producing region of northern Spain adjacent to, and overshadowed by, Rioja. Navarra's wines can be startlingly akin to their neighbouring rivals, and sometimes rather better value for money.

négociant – In France, a dealer-producer who buys wines from growers and matures and/or blends them for sale under his own label. Purists can be a bit sniffy about these entrepreneurs, claiming that only the vine-grower with his or her own winemaking set-up can make truly authentic stuff, but the truth is that many of the best wines of France are négociant-produced – especially at the humbler end of the price scale. Négociants are often identified on wine labels as négociant-éleveur (literally 'dealer-bringer-up') and meaning that the wine has been matured, blended and bottled by the party in question.

Negroamaro – Black grape variety mainly of Apulia, the fast-improving wine region of south-east Italy. Dense, earthy red wines with ageing potential and plenty of alcohol. The grape behind Copertino.

Nerello Mascalese – Black grape of Sicily making light, flavoursome and alcoholic reds.

Nero d'Avola – Black grape variety of Sicily and southern Italy. It makes deep-coloured wines that, given half a chance, can develop intensity and richness with age.

non-vintage – A wine is described as such when it has been blended from the harvests of more than one year. A non-vintage wine is not necessarily an inferior one, but under quality-control regulations around the world, still table wines most usually derive solely from one year's grape crop to qualify for appellation status. Champagnes and sparkling wines are mostly blended from several vintages, as are fortified wines, such as basic port and sherry.

nose – In the vocabulary of the wine-taster, the nose is the scent of a wine. Sounds a bit dotty, but it makes a sensible enough alternative to the rather bald 'smell'. The use of the word 'perfume' implies that the wine smells particularly good. 'Aroma' is used specifically to describe a wine that smells as it should, as in 'this burgundy has the authentic strawberry-raspberry aroma of Pinot Noir'.

O

oak – Most of the world's most expensive wines are matured in new or nearly new oak barrels, giving additional opulence of flavour. Of late, many cheaper wines have been getting the oak treatment, too, in older, cheaper casks, or simply by having sacks of oak chippings poured into their steel or fibreglass holding tanks. 'Oak aged' on a label is likely to indicate the latter treatments. But the overtly oaked wines of Australia have in some cases been so overdone that there is now a reactive trend whereby some producers proclaim their wines – particularly Chardonnays – as 'unoaked' on the label, thereby asserting that the flavours are more naturally achieved.

Oltrepo Pavese – Wine-producing zone of Piedmont, north-west Italy. The name means 'south of Pavia across the [river] Po' and the wines, both white and red, can be excellent quality and value for money.

organic wine – As in other sectors of the food industry, demand for organically made wine is – or appears to be – growing. As a rule, a wine qualifies as organic if it comes entirely from grapes grown in vineyards cultivated without the use of synthetic materials, and made in a winery where chemical treatments or additives are shunned with similar vigour. In fact, there are plenty of winemakers in the world using organic methods, but who disdain to label their bottles as such. Wines proclaiming their organic status used to carry the same sort of premium as their counterparts round the corner in the fruit, vegetable and meat aisles. But organic viticulture is now commonplace and there seems little price impact. There is no single worldwide (or even Europe-wide) standard for organic food or wine, so you pretty much have to take the producer's word for it.

P

Pasqua – One of the biggest and, it should be said, best wine producers of the Veneto region of north-west Italy.

Passetoutgrains – Bourgogne passetoutgrains is a generic appellation of the Burgundy region, France. The word loosely means 'any grapes allowed' and is supposed specifically to designate a red wine made with Gamay grapes as well as Burgundy's principal black variety, Pinot Noir, in a ratio of two parts Gamay to one of Pinot. The wine is usually relatively inexpensive, and relatively uninteresting, too.

Periquita – Black grape variety of southern Portugal. Makes rather exotic spicy reds. Name means 'parrot'.

Petit Verdot – Black grape variety of Bordeaux used to give additional colour, density and spiciness to Cabernet Sauvignon-dominated blends. Mostly a minority player at home, but in Australia and California it is grown as the principal variety for some big hearty reds of real character.

petrol – When white wines from certain grapes, especially Riesling, are allowed to age in the bottle for longer than a year or two, they can take on a spiry aroma reminiscent of petrol or diesel. In grand mature German wines, this is considered a very good thing.

Picpoul – Grape variety of southern France. Best known in Picpoul de Pinet, a dry white from near Carcassonne in the Languedoc. The name Picpoul means 'stings the lips' – referring to the natural high acidity of the juice.

Piemonte – North-western province of Italy, which we call Piedmont, known for the spumante wines of the town of Asti, plus expensive Barbaresco and Barolo and better-value varietal red wines from Barbera and Dolcetto grapes.

Pinotage – South Africa's own black grape variety. Makes red wines ranging from light and juicy to dark, strong and long-lived. It's a cross between Pinot Noir and a grape the South Africans used to call Hermitage (thus the portmanteau name) but turns out to have been Cinsault.

Pinot Blanc – White grape variety principally of Alsace, France. Florally perfumed, exotically fruity dry white wines.

Pinot Grigio – White grape variety of northern Italy. Wines bearing its name are perplexingly fashionable. Good examples have an interesting smoky-pungent aroma and keen, slaking fruit. But most are dull. Originally French, it is at its best in the lushly exotic Pinot Gris wines of Alsace.

Pinot Noir – The great black grape of Burgundy, France. It makes all the region's fabulously expensive red wines. Notoriously difficult to grow in warmer climates, it is nevertheless cultivated by countless intrepid winemakers in the New World intent on reproducing the magic appeal of red burgundy. California and New Zealand have come closest, but rarely at prices much below those for the real thing. Some Chilean Pinot Noirs are inexpensive and worth trying.

Pouilly Fuissé – Village and AC of the Mâconnais region of southern Burgundy in France. Dry white wines from Chardonnay grapes. Wines are among the highest rated of the Mâconnais.

Pouilly Fumé – Village and AC of the Loire Valley in France. Dry white wines from Sauvignon Blanc grapes. Similar 'pebbly', 'grassy' or even 'gooseberry' style to neighbouring AC Sancerre. The notion put about by some enthusiasts that Pouilly Fumé is 'smoky' is surely nothing more than word association with the name.

Primitivo – Black grape variety of southern Italy, especially the region of Puglia. Named from Latin primus for first, the grape is among the earliest-ripening of all varieties. The wines are typically dense and dark in colour with plenty of alcohol, and have an earthy, spicy style. Often a real bargain.

Prosecco – White grape variety of Italy's Veneto region known entirely for the softly sparkling wine it makes. The best come from the DOC Conegliano-Valdobbiadene, made as spumante ('foaming') wines in pressurised tanks, typically to 11 per cent alcohol and ranging from softly sweet to crisply dry. Now trendy, but the cheap wines – one leading brand comes in a can – are of very variable quality.

Puglia – The region occupying the 'heel' of southern Italy, lately making many good, inexpensive wines from indigenous grape varieties.

Q

QbA – German, standing for Qualitätswein bestimmter Anbaugebiete. It means 'quality wine from designated areas' and implies that the wine is made from grapes with a minimum level of ripeness, but it's by no means a guarantee of exciting quality. Only wines labelled QmP (see next entry) can be depended upon to be special.

QmP – Stands for Qualitätswein mit Prädikat. These are the serious wines of Germany, made without the addition of sugar to 'improve' them. To qualify for QmP status, the grapes must reach a level of ripeness as measured on a sweetness scale – all according to Germany's fiendishly complicated wine-quality regulations. Wines from grapes that reach the stated minimum level of sweetness qualify for the description of Kabinett. The next level up earns the rank of Spätlese, meaning 'late-picked'. Kabinett wines can be expected to be dry and brisk in style, and Spätlese wines a little bit riper and fuller. The next grade up, Auslese, meaning 'selected harvest', indicates a wine made from super-ripe grapes; it will be golden in colour and honeyed in flavour. A generation ago, these wines were as valued, and as expensive, as any of the world's grandest appellations, but the collapse in demand for German wines in the UK – brought about by the disrepute rightly earned for floods of filthy Liebfraumilch – means they are now seriously undervalued.

Quincy – AC of Loire Valley, France, known for pebbly-dry white wines from Sauvignon grapes. The wines are forever compared to those of nearby and much better-known Sancerre – and Quincy often represents better value for money. Pronounced 'KAN-see'.

Quinta – Portuguese for farm or estate. It precedes the names of many of Portugal's best-known wines. It is pronounced 'KEEN-ta'.

R

racy – Evocative wine-tasting description for wine that thrills the tastebuds with a rush of exciting sensations. Good Rieslings often qualify.

raisiny – Wines from grapes that have been very ripe or overripe at harvest can take on a smell and flavour akin to the concentrated, heat-dried sweetness of raisins. As a minor element in the character of a wine, this can add to the appeal but as a dominant characteristic it is a fault.

rancio – Spanish term harking back to Roman times when wines were commonly stored in jars outside, exposed to the sun, so they oxidised and took on a burnt sort of flavour. Today, rancio describes a baked – and by no means unpleasant – flavour in fortified wines, particularly sherry and Madeira.

Reserva – In Portugal and Spain, this has genuine significance. The Portuguese use it for special wines with a higher alcohol level and longer ageing, although the precise periods vary between regions. In Spain, especially in the Navarra and Rioja regions, it means the wine must have had at least a year in oak and two in bottle before release.

reserve – On French (as réserve) or other wines, this implies special-quality, longer-aged wines, but has no official significance.

Retsina – The universal white wine of Greece. It has been traditionally made in Attica, the region of Athens, for a very long time, and is said to owe its origins and name to the ancient custom of sealing amphorae (terracotta jars) of the wine with a gum made from pine resin. Some of the flavour of the resin inevitably transmitted itself into the wine, and ancient Greeks acquired a lasting taste for it.

Reuilly – AC of Loire Valley, France, for crisp dry whites from Sauvignon grapes. Pronounced 'RER-yee'.

Ribatejo – Emerging wine region of Portugal. Worth seeking out on labels of red wines in particular, because new winemakers are producing lively stuff from distinctive indigenous grapes such as Castelao and Trincadeira.

Ribera del Duero – Classic wine region of north-west Spain lying along the River Duero (which crosses the border to become Portugal's Douro, forming the valley where port comes from). It is home to an estate rather oddly named Vega Sicilia, where red wines of epic quality are made and sold at equally epic prices. Further down the scale, some very good reds are made, too.

Riesling – The noble grape variety of Germany. It is correctly pronounced 'REEZ-ling', not 'RICE-ling'. Once notorious as the grape behind all those boring 'medium' Liebfraumilches and Niersteiners, this grape has had a bad press. In fact, there has never been much, if any, Riesling in Germany's cheap-and-nasty plonks. But the country's best wines, the so-called Qualitätswein mit Prädikat grades, are made almost exclusively with Riesling. These wines range from crisply fresh and appley styles to extravagantly fruity, honeyed wines from late-harvested grapes. Excellent Riesling wines are also made in Alsace and now in Australia.

Rioja – The principal fine-wine region of Spain, in the country's north east. The pricier wines are noted for their vanilla-pod richness from long ageing in oak casks. Tempranillo and Garnacha grapes make the reds, Viura the whites.

Ripasso – A particular style of Valpolicella wine. New wine is partially refermented in vats that have been used to make the recioto reds (wines made from semi-dried grapes), thus creating a bigger, smoother version of usually light and pale Valpolicella.

Riserva – In Italy, a wine made only in the best vintages, and allowed longer ageing in cask and bottle.

Rivaner – Alternative name for Germany's Müller-Thurgau grape, the life-blood of Liebfraumilch.

Riverland – Vineyard region to the immediate north of the Barossa Valley of South Australia, extending east into New South Wales.

Roditis – White grape variety of Greece, known for fresh dry whites with decent acidity, often included in retsina.

rosso – Red wine, Italy.

Rosso Conero – DOC red wine made in the environs of Ancona in the Marches, Italy. Made from the Montepulciano grape, the wine can provide excellent value for money.

Ruby Cabernet – Black grape variety of California, created by crossing Cabernet Sauvignon and Carignan. Makes soft and squelchy red wine at home and in South Africa.

Rueda – DO of north-west Spain making first-class refreshing dry whites from the indigenous Verdejo grape, imported Sauvignon, and others. Exciting quality, and prices are keen.

Rully – AC of Chalonnais region of southern Burgundy, France. White wines from Chardonnay and red wines from Pinot Noir grapes. Both can be very good and are substantially cheaper than their more northerly Burgundian neighbours. Pronounced 'ROO-yee'.

S

Saint Emilion – AC of Bordeaux, France. Centred on the romantic hill town of St Emilion, this famous sub-region makes some of the grandest red wines of France, but also some of the best-value ones. Less fashionable than the Médoc region on the opposite (west) bank of the River Gironde that bisects Bordeaux, St Emilion wines are made largely with the Merlot grape, and are relatively quick to mature. The grandest wines are classified 1er grand cru classé and are madly expensive, but many more are classified respectively grand cru classé and grand cru, and these designations can be seen as a fairly trustworthy indicator of quality. There are several 'satellite' St Emilion ACs named after the villages at their centres, notably Lussac St Emilion, Montagne St Emilion and Puisseguin St Emilion. Some excellent wines are made by estates within these ACs, and at relatively affordable prices thanks to the comparatively humble status of their satellite designations.

Salento – Up-and-coming wine region of southern Italy. Many good bargain reds from local grapes including Nero d'Avola and Primitivo.

Sancerre – AC of the Loire Valley, France, renowned for flinty-fresh Sauvignon whites and rarer Pinot Noir reds. These wines are never cheap, and recent tastings make it plain that only the best-made, individual-producer wines are worth the money. Budget brands seem mostly dull.

Sangiovese – The local black grape of Tuscany, Italy. It is the principal variety used for Chianti and is now widely planted in Latin America – often making delicious, Chianti-like wines with characteristic cherryish-but-deeply-ripe fruit and a dry, clean finish. Chianti wines have become (unjustifiably) expensive in recent years and cheaper Italian wines such as those called Sangiovese di Toscana make a consoling substitute.

Saumur – Town and appellation of Loire Valley, France. Characterful minerally red wines from Cabernet Franc grapes, and some whites. The once-popular sparkling wines from Chenin Blanc grapes are now little seen in Britain.

Saumur-Champigny – Separate appellation for red wines from Cabernet Franc grapes of Saumur in the Loire, sometimes very good and lively.

Sauvignon Blanc – French white grape variety now grown worldwide. New Zealand is successfully challenging the long supremacy of French ACs such as Sancerre. The wines are characterised by aromas of gooseberry, fresh-cut grass, even asparagus. Flavours are often described as 'grassy' or 'nettly'.

sec – Dry wine style. French.

secco – Dry wine style. Italian.

Semillon – White grape variety originally of Bordeaux, where it is blended with Sauvignon Blanc to make fresh dry whites and, when harvested very late in the season, the ambrosial sweet whites of Barsac, Sauternes and other appellations. Even in the driest wines, the grape can be recognised from its honeyed, sweet-pineapple, even banana-like aromas. Now widely planted in Australia and Latin America, and frequently blended with Chardonnay to make dry whites, some of them interesting.

sherry – The great aperitif wine of Spain, centred on the Andalusian city of Jerez (from which the name 'sherry' is an English mispronunciation). There is a lot of sherry-style wine in the world, but only the authentic wine from Jerez and the neighbouring producing towns of Puerta de Santa Maria and Sanlucar de Barrameda may label their wines as such. The Spanish drink real sherry – very dry and fresh, pale in colour and served well-chilled – called fino and manzanilla, and darker but naturally dry variations called amontillado, palo cortado and oloroso.

Shiraz – Australian name for the Syrah grape. The variety is the most widely planted of any in Australia, and makes red wines of wildly varying quality, characterised by dense colour, high alcohol, spicy fruit and generous, cushiony texture.

Somontano – Wine region of north-east Spain. Name means 'under the mountains' – in this case the Pyrenees – and the region has had DO status since 1984. Much innovative winemaking here, with New World styles emerging. Some very good buys. A region to watch.

souple – French wine-tasting term that translates into English as 'supple' or even 'docile' as in 'pliable', but I understand it in the vinous context to mean muscular but soft – a wine with tannin as well as soft fruit.

Spätlese – See QmP.

spirity – Some wines, mostly from the New World, are made from grapes so ripe at harvest that their high alcohol content can be detected through a mildly burning sensation on the tongue, similar to the effect of sipping a spirit.

spritzy – Describes a wine with a barely detectable sparkle. Some young wines are intended to have this elusive fizziness; in others it is a fault.

spumante – Sparkling wine of Italy. Asti Spumante is the best known, from the town of Asti in the north-west Italian province of Piemonte. The term describes wines that are fully sparkling. Frizzante wines have a less vigorous mousse.

stalky – A useful tasting term to describe red wines with flavours that make you think the stalks from the grape bunches must have been fermented along with the must (juice). Young Bordeaux reds very often have this mild astringency. In moderation it's fine, but if it dominates it probably signifies the wine is at best immature and at worst badly made.

Stellenbosch – Town and region at the heart of South Africa's burgeoning wine industry. It's an hour's drive from Cape Town and the source of much of the country's cheaper wine. Quality is variable, and the name Stellenbosch on a label can't (yet, anyway) be taken as a guarantee of quality.

stony – Wine-tasting term for keenly dry white wines. It's meant to indicate a wine of purity and real quality, with just the right match of fruit and acidity.

structured – Good wines are not one-dimensional, they have layers of flavour and texture. A structured wine has phases of enjoyment: the 'attack', or first impression in the mouth; the middle palate as the wine is held in the mouth; and the lingering aftertaste.

summer fruit – Wine-tasting term intended to convey a smell or taste of soft fruits such as strawberries and raspberries – without having to commit too specifically to which.

Superiore – On labels of Italian wines, this is more than an idle boast. Under DOC rules, wines must qualify for the superiore designation by reaching one or more specified quality levels, usually a higher alcohol content or an additional period of maturation. Frascati, for example, qualifies for DOC status at 11.5 per cent alcohol, but to be classified superiore must have 12 per cent alcohol.

sur lie – Literally, 'on the lees'. It's a term now widely used on the labels of Muscadet wines, signifying that after fermentation has died down, the new wine has been left in the tank over the winter on the lees – the detritus of yeasts and other interesting compounds left over from the turbid fermentation process. The idea is that additional interest is imparted into the flavour of the wine.

Syrah – The noble grape of the Rhône Valley, France. Makes very dark, dense wine characterised by peppery, tarry aromas. Now planted all over southern France and farther afield. In Australia, where it makes wines ranging from disagreeably jam-like plonks to wonderfully rich and silky keeping wines, it is known as Shiraz.

T

table wine – Wine that is unfortified and of an alcoholic strength, for UK tax purposes anyway, of no more than 15 per cent. I use the term to distinguish, for example, between the red table wines of the Douro Valley in Portugal and the region's better-known fortified wine, port.

Tafelwein – Table wine, German. The humblest quality designation, which doesn't usually bode very well.

tank method – Bulk-production process for sparkling wines. Base wine undergoes secondary fermentation in a large, sealed vat rather than in individual closed bottles. Also known as the Charmat method after the name of the inventor of the process.

Tannat – Black grape of south-west France, notably for wines of Madiran, and lately named as the variety most beneficial to health thanks to its outstanding antioxidant content.

tannin – Well known as the film-forming, teeth-coating component in tea, tannin is a natural compound that occurs in black grape skins and acts as a natural preservative in wine. Its noticeable presence in wine is regarded as a good thing. It gives young everyday reds their dryness, firmness of flavour and backbone. And it helps high-quality reds to retain their lively fruitiness for many years. A grand Bordeaux red when first made, for example, will have purply-sweet, rich fruit and mouth-puckering tannin, but after ten years or so this will have evolved into a delectably fruity, mature wine in which the formerly parching effects of the tannin have receded almost completely, leaving the shade of 'residual tannin' that marks out a great wine approaching maturity.

Tarrango – Black grape variety of Australia.

tarry – On the whole, winemakers don't like critics to say their wines evoke the redolence of road repairs, but I can't help using this term to describe the agreeable, sweet, 'burnt' flavour that is often found at the centre of the fruit in wines from Argentina, Italy and Portugal in particular.

TCA – Dreaded ailment in wine, usually blamed on faulty corks. It stands for 246 *trichloroanisol* and is characterised by a horrible musty smell and flavour in the affected wine. It is largely because of the current plague of TCA that so many wine producers worldwide are now going over to polymer 'corks' and screwcaps.

tears – The colourless alcohol in the wine left clinging to the inside of the glass after the contents have been swirled. Persistent tears (also known as 'legs') indicate a wine of good concentration.

Tempranillo – The great black grape of Spain. Along with Garnacha (Grenache in France) it makes all red Rioja and Navarra wines and, under many pseudonyms, is an important or exclusive contributor to the wines of many other regions of Spain. It is also widely cultivated in South America.

tinto – On Spanish labels indicates a deeply coloured red wine. Clarete denotes a paler colour. Also Portuguese.

Toro – Quality wine region east of Zamora, Spain.

Torrontes – White grape variety of Argentina. Makes soft, dry wines often with delicious grapey-spicy aroma, similar in style to the classic dry Muscat wines of Alsace, but at more accessible prices.

Touraine – Region encompassing a swathe of the Loire Valley, France. Non-AC wines may be labelled 'Sauvignon de Touraine' etc.

Touriga Nacional – The most valued black grape variety of the Douro Valley in Portugal, where port is made. The name Touriga now appears on an increasing number of table wines made as sidelines by the port producers. They can be very good, with the same spirity aroma and sleek flavours of port itself, minus the fortification.

Traminer – Grape variety, the same as Gewürztraminer.

Trebbiano – The workhorse white grape of Italy. A productive variety that is easy to cultivate, it seems to be included in just about every ordinary white wine of the entire nation – including Frascati, Orvieto and Soave. It is the same grape as France's Ugni Blanc. There are, however, distinct regional variations of the grape. Trebbiano di Lugana makes a distinctive white in the DOC of the name, sometimes very good, while Trebbiano di Toscana makes a major contribution to the distinctly less interesting dry whites of Chianti country.

Trincadeira Preta – Portuguese black grape variety native to the port-producing vineyards of the Douro Valley (where it goes under the name Tinta Amarella). In southern Portugal, it produces dark and sturdy table wines.

trocken – 'Dry' German wine. It's a recent trend among commercial-scale producers in the Rhine and Mosel to label their wines with this description in the hope of reassuring consumers that the contents do not resemble the dreaded sugar-water Liebfraumilch-type plonks of the bad old days. But the description does have a particular meaning under German wine law, namely that there is only a low level of unfermented sugar lingering in the wine (9 grams per litre, if you need to know), and this can leave the wine tasting rather austere.

U

Ugni Blanc – The most widely cultivated white grape variety of France and the mainstay of many a cheap dry white wine. To date it has been better known as the provider of base wine for distilling into armagnac and cognac, but lately the name has been appearing on wine labels. Technology seems to be improving the performance of the grape. The curious name is pronounced 'OON-yee', and is the same variety as Italy's ubiquitous Trebbiano.

V

Vacqueyras – Village of the southern Rhône Valley of France in the region better known for its generic appellation, the Côtes du Rhône. Vacqueyras can date its winemaking history all the way back to 1414, but has only been producing under its own village AC since 1991. The wines, from Grenache and Syrah grapes, can be wonderfully silky and intense, spicy and long-lived.

Valdepeñas – An island of quality production amidst the ocean of mediocrity that is Spain's La Mancha region – where most of the grapes are grown for distilling into the head-banging brandies of Jerez. Valdepeñas reds are made from a grape they call the Cencibel – which turns out to be a very close relation of the Tempranillo grape that is the mainstay of the fine but expensive red wines of Rioja. Again, like Rioja, Valdepeñas wines are matured in oak casks to give them a vanilla-rich smoothness. Among bargain reds, Valdepeñas is a name to look out for.

Valpolicella – Red wine of Verona, Italy. Good examples have ripe, cherry fruit and a pleasingly dry finish. Unfortunately, there are many bad examples of Valpolicella. Shop with circumspection. Valpolicella Classico wines, from the best vineyards clustered around the town, are more reliable. Those additionally labelled Superiore have higher alcohol and some bottle age.

vanilla – Ageing wines in oak barrels (or, less picturesquely, adding oak chips to wine in huge concrete vats) imparts a range of characteristics including a smell of vanilla from the ethyl vanilline naturally given off by oak.

varietal – A varietal wine is one named after the grape variety (one or more) from which it is made. Nearly all everyday wines worldwide are now labelled in this way. It is salutary to contemplate that just 30 years ago, wines described thus were virtually unknown outside Germany and one or two quirky regions of France and Italy.

vegan-friendly – My informal way of noting that a wine is claimed to have been made not only with animal-product-free finings (see Vegetarian wine) but without any animal-related products whatsoever, such as manure in the vineyards.

vegetal – A tasting note definitely open to interpretation. It suggests a smell or flavour reminiscent less of fruit (apple, pineapple, strawberry and the like) than of something leafy or even root based. Some wines are evocative (to some tastes) of beetroot, cabbage or even unlikelier vegetable flavours – and these characteristics may add materially to the attraction of the wine.

vegetarian wine – Wines labelled 'suitable for vegetarians' have been made without the assistance of animal products for 'fining'

– clarifying – before bottling. Gelatine, egg whites, isinglass from fish bladders and casein from milk are among the items shunned, usually in favour of bentonite, an absorbent clay first found at Benton in the US state of Montana.

Verdejo – White grape of the Rueda region in north-west Spain. It can make superbly perfumed crisp dry whites of truly distinctive character and has helped make Rueda one of the best white-wine sources of Europe. No relation to Verdelho.

Verdelho – Portuguese grape variety once mainly used for a medium-dry style of Madeira, also called Verdelho, but now rare. The vine is now prospering in Australia, where it can make well-balanced dry whites with fleeting richness and lemon-lime acidity.

Verdicchio – White grape variety of Italy best known in the DOC zone of Castelli dei Jesi in the Adriatic wine region of the Marches. Dry white wines once known for little more than their naff amphora-style bottles but now gaining a reputation for interesting, herbaceous flavours of recognisable character.

Vermentino – White grape variety principally of Italy, especially Sardinia. Makes florally scented soft dry whites.

Vieilles vignes – Old vines. Many French producers like to claim on their labels that the wine within is from vines of notable antiquity. While it's true that vines don't produce useful grapes for the first few years after planting, it is uncertain whether vines of much greater age – say 25 years plus – than others actually make better fruit. There are no regulations governing the use of the term, so it's not a reliable indicator anyway.

Vin Délimité de Qualité Supérieure – Usually abbreviated to VDQS, a French wine-quality designation between appellation contrôlée and vin de pays. To qualify, the wine has to be from approved grape varieties grown in a defined zone. This designation is gradually disappearing.

vin de liqueur – Sweet style of white wine mostly from the Pyrenean region of south-westernmost France, made by adding a little spirit to the new wine before it has fermented out, halting the fermentation and retaining sugar.

vin de pays – 'Country wine' of France. The French map is divided up into more than 100 vin de pays regions. Wine in bottles labelled as such must be from grapes grown in the nominated zone or département. Some vin de pays areas are huge: the Vin de Pays d'Oc (named after the Languedoc region) covers much of the Midi and Provence. Plenty of wines bearing this humble designation are of astoundingly high quality and certainly compete with New World counterparts for interest and value.

Vin de Pays d'Oc – Largest of the zones, encompasses much of the huge region of the Languedoc of south-west France. Many excellent wines are sold under this classification, particularly those made in appellation areas from grapes not permitted locally.

vin de table – The humblest official classification of French wine. Neither the region, grape varieties nor vintage need be stated on the label. The wine might not even be French. Don't expect too much from this kind of 'table wine'.

vin doux naturel – Sweet, mildly fortified wine of southern France. A little spirit is added during the winemaking process, halting the fermentation by killing the yeast before it has consumed all the sugars – hence the pronounced sweetness of the wine.

vin gris – Rosé wine from Provence.

Vinho de mesa – 'Table wine' of Portugal.

Vino da tavola – The humblest official classification of Italian wine. Much ordinary plonk bears this designation, but the bizarre quirks of Italy's wine laws dictate that some of that country's finest wines are also classed as mere vino da tavola (table wine). If an expensive Italian wine is labelled as such, it doesn't mean it will be a disappointment.

Vino de mesa – 'Table wine' of Spain. Usually very ordinary.

vintage – The grape harvest. The year displayed on bottle labels is the year of the harvest. Wines bearing no date have been blended from the harvests of two or more years.

Viognier – A grape variety once exclusive to the northern Rhône Valley in France where it makes a very chi-chi wine, Condrieu, usually costing £20 plus. Now, the Viognier is grown more widely, in North and South

America as well as elsewhere in France, and occasionally produces soft, marrowy whites that echo the grand style of Condrieu itself. The Viognier is now commonly blended with Shiraz in red winemaking in Australia and South Africa. It does not dilute the colour and is confidently believed by highly experienced winemakers to enhance the quality. Steve Webber, in charge of winemaking at the revered De Bortoli estates in the Yarra Valley region of Victoria, Australia, puts between two and five per cent Viognier in with some of his Shiraz wines. 'I think it's the perfume,' he told me. 'It gives some femininity to the wine.'

Viura – White grape variety of Rioja, Spain. Also widely grown elsewhere in Spain under the name Macabeo. Wines have a blossomy aroma and are dry, but sometimes soft at the expense of acidity.

Vouvray – AC of the Loire Valley, France, known for still and sparkling dry white wines and sweet, still whites from late-harvested grapes. The wines, all from Chenin Blanc grapes, have a unique capacity for unctuous softness combined with lively freshness – an effect best portrayed in the demi-sec (slightly sweet) wines, which can be delicious and keenly priced. Unfashionable, but worth looking out for.

Vranac – Black grape variety of the Balkans known for dense colour and tangy-bitter edge to the flavour. Best enjoyed in situ.

W

weight – In an ideal world the weight of a wine is determined by the ripeness of the grapes from which it has been made. In some cases the weight is determined merely by the quantity of sugar added during the production process. A good, genuine wine described as having weight is one in which there is plenty of alcohol and 'extract' – colour and flavour from the grapes. Wine enthusiasts judge weight by swirling the wine in the glass and then examining the 'legs' or 'tears' left clinging to the inside of the glass after the contents have subsided. Alcohol gives these runlets a dense, glycerine-like condition, and if they cling for a long time, the wine is deemed to have weight – a very good thing in all honestly made wines.

Winzergenossenschaft – One of the many very lengthy and peculiar words regularly found on labels of German wines. This means a winemaking co-operative. Many excellent German wines are made by these associations of growers.

woodsap – A subjective tasting note. Some wines have a fleeting bitterness, which is not a fault, but an interesting balancing factor amidst very ripe flavours. The effect somehow evokes woodsap.

X

Xarel-lo – One of the main grape varieties for cava, the sparkling wine of Spain.

Xinomavro – Black grape variety of Greece. It retains its acidity even in the very hot conditions that prevail in many Greek vineyards, where harvests tend to over-ripen and make cooked-tasting wines. Modern winemaking techniques are capable of making well-balanced wines from Xinomavro.

Y

Yecla – Town and DO wine region of eastern Spain, close to Alicante, making lots of interesting, strong-flavoured red and white wines, often at bargain prices.

yellow – White wines are not white at all, but various shades of yellow – or, more poetically, gold. Some white wines with opulent richness even have a flavour I cannot resist calling yellow – reminiscent of butter.

Z

Zinfandel – Black grape variety of California. Makes brambly reds, some of which can age very gracefully, and 'blush' whites – actually pink, because a little of the skin colour is allowed to leach into the must. The vine is also planted in Australia and South America. The Primitivo of southern Italy is said to be a related variety, but makes a very different kind of wine.

—Making the most of it—

There has always been a lot of nonsense talked about the correct ways to serve wine. Red wine, we are told, should be opened and allowed to 'breathe' before pouring. White wine should be chilled. Wine doesn't go with soup, tomatoes or chocolate. You know the sort of thing.

It would all be simply laughable except that these daft conventions do make so many potential wine lovers nervous about the simple ritual of opening a bottle and sharing it around. Here is a short and opinionated guide to the received wisdom.

Breathing

Simply uncorking a wine for an hour or two before you serve it will make absolutely no difference to the way it tastes. However, if you wish to warm up an icy bottle of red by placing it near (never on) a radiator or fire, do remove the cork first. As the wine warms, even very slightly, it gives off gas, which will spoil the flavour if it cannot escape.

Chambré-ing

One of the more florid terms in the wine vocabulary. The idea is that red wine should be at the same temperature as the room (chambre) you're going to drink it in. In fairness, it makes sense – although the term harks back to the days when the only people who drank wine were those who could afford to keep it in the freezing cold vaulted cellars beneath their houses. The ridiculously high temperatures to which some homes are raised by central heating systems today are really far too warm for wine. But presumably those who live in such circumstances do so out of choice, and will prefer their wine to be similarly overheated.

Chilling

Drink your white wine as cold as you like. It's certainly true that good whites are at their best at a cool rather than at an icy temperature, but cheap and characterless wines can be improved immeasurably if they are cold enough – the anaesthetising effect of the temperature removes all sense of taste. Pay no attention to notions that red wine should not be served cool. There are plenty of lightweight reds that will respond very well to an hour in the fridge.

Corked wine

Wine trade surveys reveal that far too many bottles are in no fit state to be sold. The villain is very often cited as the cork. Cut from the bark of cork-oak trees cultivated for the purpose in Portugal and Spain, these natural stoppers have done sterling service for 200 years, but now face a crisis of confidence among wine producers. A diseased or damaged cork can make the wine taste stale because air has penetrated, or musty-mushroomy due to TCA, an infection of the raw material. These faults in wine, known as 'corked' or 'corky', should be immediately obvious, even in the humblest bottle, so you should return the bottle to the supplier and demand a refund.

Today, more and more wine producers are opting to close their bottles with polymer bungs. Some are designed to resemble the 'real thing' while others come in a rather disorienting range of colours – including black. While these things can be a pain to extract, there seems to be no evidence they do any harm to the wine. Don't 'lay down' bottles closed with polymer. The potential effects of years of contact with the plastic are yet to be scientifically established.

The same goes for screwcaps. These do have the merit of obviating the struggle with the corkscrew, but prolonged contact of the plastic liner with the wine might not be a good idea.

Corkscrews

The best kind of corkscrew is the 'waiter's friend' type. It looks like a pen-knife, unfolding a 'worm' (the helix or screw) and a lever device which, after the worm has been driven into the cork (try to centre it) rests on the lip of the bottle and enables you to withdraw the cork with minimal effort. Some have two-stage lips to facilitate the task. These devices are cheaper and longer-lasting than any of the more elaborate types, and are equally effective at withdrawing polymer bungs – which can be hellishly difficult to unwind from Teflon-coated 'continuous' corkscrews like the Screwpull.

Decanting

There are two views on the merits of decanting wines. The prevailing one seems to be that it is pointless and even pretentious. The other is that it can make real improvements in the way a wine tastes and is definitely worth the trouble.

Scientists, not usually much exercised by the finer nuances of wine, will tell you that exposure to the air causes wine to 'oxidise' – take in oxygen molecules that will quite quickly initiate the process of turning wine into vinegar – and anyone who has tasted a 'morning-after' glass of wine will no doubt vouch for this.

But the fact that wine does oxidise is a genuine clue to the reality of the effects of exposure to air. Shut inside its bottle, a young wine is very much a live substance, jumping with natural, but mysterious, compounds that can cause all sorts of strange taste sensations. But by exposing the wine to air these effects are markedly reduced.

In wines that spend longer in the bottle, the influence of these factors diminishes, in a process called 'reduction'. In red wines, the hardness of tannin – the natural preservative imparted into wine from the grape skins – gradually reduces, just as the raw purple colour darkens to ruby and later to orangey-brown.

I believe there is less reason for decanting old wines than new, unless the old wine has thrown a deposit and needs carefully to be poured off it. And in some light-bodied wines, such as older Rioja, decanting is probably a bad idea because it can accelerate oxidation all too quickly.

As to actual experiments, I have carried out several of my own, with wines opened in advance or wines decanted compared to the same wines just opened and poured, and my own unscientific judgement is that big, young, alcoholic reds can certainly be improved by aeration.

Washing glasses

If your wine glasses are of any value to you, don't put them in the dishwasher. Over time, they'll craze from the heat of the water. And they will not emerge in the glitteringly pristine condition suggested by the pictures on some detergent packets. For genuinely perfect glasses that will stay that way, wash them in hot soapy water, rinse with clean, hot water and dry immediately with a glass cloth kept exclusively for this purpose. Sounds like fanaticism, but if you take your wine seriously, you'll see there is sense in it.

Keeping wine

How long can you keep an opened bottle of wine before it goes downhill? Not long. A re-corked bottle with just a glassful out of it should stay fresh until the day after, but if there is a lot of air inside the bottle, the wine will oxidise, turning progressively stale and sour. Wine 'saving' devices that allow you to withdraw the air from the bottle via a punctured, self-sealing rubber stopper are variably effective, but don't expect these to keep a wine fresh for more than a couple of re-openings. A crafty method of keeping a half-finished bottle is to decant it, via a funnel, into a clean half bottle and recork.

Storing wine

Supermarket labels always seem to advise that 'this wine should be consumed within one year of purchase'. I think this is a wheeze to persuade customers to drink it up quickly and come back for more. Many of the more robust red wines are likely to stay in good condition for much more than one year, and plenty will actually improve with age. On the other hand, it is a sensible axiom that inexpensive dry white wines are better the younger they are. If you do intend to store wines for longer than a few weeks, do pay heed to the conventional wisdom that bottles are best stored in low, stable temperatures, preferably in the dark. Bottles closed with conventional corks should be laid on their side lest the corks dry out for lack of contact with the wine. But one of the notable advantages of the new closures now proliferating is that if your wine comes with a polymer 'cork' or a screwcap, you can safely store it upright.

Wine and food

Wine is made to be drunk with food, but some wines go better with particular dishes than others. It is no coincidence that Italian wines, characterised by soft, cherry fruit and a clean, mouth-drying finish, go so well with the sticky delights of pasta.

But it's personal taste rather than national associations that should determine the choice of wine with food. And if you prefer a black-hearted Argentinian Malbec to a brambly Italian Barbera with your Bolognese, that's fine.

The conventions that have grown up around wine and food pairings do make some sense, just the same. I was thrilled to learn in the early days of my drinking career that sweet, dessert wines can go well with strong blue cheese. As I don't much like puddings, but love sweet wines, I was eager to test this match – and I'm here to tell you that it works very well indeed as the end-piece to a grand meal in which there is cheese as well as pud on offer.

Red wine and cheese are supposed to be a natural match, but I'm not so sure. Reds can taste awfully tinny with soft cheeses such as Brie and Camembert, and even worse with goat's cheese. A really extravagant, yellow Australian Chardonnay will make a better match. Hard cheeses such as Cheddar and the wonderful Old Amsterdam (top-of-the-market Gouda) are better with reds.

And then there's the delicate issue of fish. Red wine is supposed to be a no-no. This might well be true of grilled and wholly unadorned white fish, such as sole or a delicate dish of prawns, scallops or crab. But what about oven-roasted monkfish or a substantial winter-season fish pie? An edgy red will do very well indeed, and provide much comfort for those many among us who simply prefer to drink red wine with food, and white wine on its own.

It is very often the method by which dishes are prepared, rather than their core ingredients, that determines which wine will work best. To be didactic, I would always choose Beaujolais or summer-fruit-style reds such as those from Pinot Noir grapes to go with a simple roast chicken. But if the bird is cooked as coq au vin with a hefty wine sauce, I would plump for a much more assertive red.

Some sauces, it is alleged, will overwhelm all wines. Salsa and curry come to mind. I have carried out a number of experiments into this great issue of our time, in my capacity as consultant to a company that specialises in supplying wines to Asian restaurants. One discovery I have made is that forcefully fruity dry white wines with keen acidity can go very well indeed even with fairly incendiary dishes. Sauvignon Blanc with Madras? Give it a try!

I'm also convinced, however, that some red wines will stand up very well to a bit of heat. The marvellously robust reds of Argentina made from Malbec grapes are good partners to Mexican chilli-hot recipes and salsa dishes. The dry, tannic edge to these wines provides a good counterpoint to the inflammatory spices in the food.

Some foods are supposedly impossible to match with wine. Eggs and chocolate are among the prime offenders. And yet, legendary cook Elizabeth David's best-selling autobiography was entitled *An Omelette and a Glass of Wine*, and the affiliation between chocolates and champagne is an unbreakable one. Taste is, after all, that most personally governed of all senses. If your choice is a boiled egg washed down with a glass of claret, who is to dictate otherwise?

Index